OUT OF SEASON

Out of Season

Sermons in Ordinary Time

LUKE TIMOTHY JOHNSON

CASCADE *Books* · Eugene, Oregon

OUT OF SEASON
Sermons in Ordinary Time

Cascade Books
An Imprint of Wipf and Stock Publishers
199 W. 8th Ave., Suite 3
Eugene, OR 97401

www.wipfandstock.com

PAPERBACK ISBN: 978-1-6667-1991-8
HARDCOVER ISBN: 978-1-6667-1992-5
EBOOK ISBN: 978-1-6667-1993-2

Cataloguing-in-Publication data:

Names: Johnson, Luke Timothy, author.

Title: Out of season : sermons in ordinary time / by Luke Timothy Johnson.

Description: Eugene, OR: Cascade Books, 2021 | Includes bibliographical references.

Identifiers: ISBN 978-1-6667-1991-8 (paperback) | ISBN 978-1-6667-1992-5 (hardcover) | ISBN 978-1-6667-1993-2 (ebook)

Subjects: LCSH: Church year sermons. | Sermons, American.

Classification: BX1756 J64 2022 (paperback) | BX1756 (ebook)

Scripture citations are from a variety of translations, according to the texts used by congregations. Translations were frequently altered by the author.

VERSION NUMBER 12/28/21

CONTENTS

WORDS AT RITUAL MOMENTS

INTRODUCTION

In Saint Paul's Second Letter to Timothy, the apostle charges his delegate to "preach the word! Be ready in season and out of season. Convince, rebuke, exhort, with all long suffering and teaching" (4:2). The venerable King James translation supplies the memorable phrase "in season and out of season" that I have appropriated as the titles of these two volumes of selected sermons. The Greek phrase used by Paul, *eukairos akairos*, had the sense of "when it is welcome and when it is not." As throughout his letter to a delegate who was prone to discouragement and even cowardice (see 1:3–8), Paul challenges Timothy to carry out his mission of preaching and teaching in every kind of circumstance, above all when people do not want to listen (4:3–4).

Modern translations have abandoned the lovely "in season and out of season" for terms that are both more precise and more intelligible to present-day readers. But while fully subscribing to Paul's urgent exhortation, I have made bold to apply the two terms in a manner he would never have anticipated. To the first volume of my selected sermons I gave the title *In Season*, because each of the homilies or sermons was connected to a moment in the church's liturgical year, and because in many of them, the liturgical moment had much to do with the character of the sermon.

For this second volume, the temptation to use the title *Out of Season* proved too great to overcome, because each homily or sermon in this selection was preached in what is called "ordinary time," that is, on occasions of worship that do not fall explicitly within the seasonal or sanctoral cycle of the liturgical year. An organizing principle for this collection was consequently less easy to determine, so I have grouped them roughly according to audience and setting: homilies to monks (when I was still a Benedictine monk), sermons to students studying for the ministry, and sermons given to scattered congregations. The final cluster consists of sermons given at ritual moments, with, as you will see, a disproportionate number preached at graduations.

In the introduction to the first volume, I recounted the way that a New Testament scholar who had never intended to be a preacher ended up writing and delivering not a few sermons over many years, first to fellow monks and congregants at Saint Joseph Abbey in Louisiana and Saint Meinrad Archabbey in Indiana, then to students and faculty at Yale Divinity School and Candler School of Theology, and finally to many congregations across the country to whom I also delivered lectures. I do not need to repeat my confession of the way that preaching—whether in a simple monastic homily or in the much grander setting of a baccalaureate—was both a source of anxiety and joy.

But one thing I can add here is the deep pleasure and satisfaction I had in struggling with the scriptural texts provided by the lectionary (which, almost without exception, I used). As I retyped the old manuscripts that had survived in a variety of ragtag folders, keeping the sermons as they were delivered and resisting the urge to improve them beyond correcting the grammar and syntax on occasion, or cutting sharper paragraphs, or replacing a too-casual word choice with a more precise diction, I was able to appreciate how many exegetical insights that later found their way into some published piece of scholarship or other had an origin in preaching. Time and again, I found myself thinking, "Wait a minute, I knew this *then*? I thought that *then*?," and found confirmed my sense that Scripture is best engaged through preaching. In this, as in so many other ways, the great Origen of Alexandria (184–254) was the model: his thousands of homilies delivered to congregations—far too few of which survive—contain the best expressions of his extraordinary mind and spirit.

Readers who might dip into more than one section of this collection will surely note a difference in tone. As I read through the sermons, I was myself struck by the simplicity and straightforwardness of the monastic homilies, where everything could be assumed among men who lived a common life, in contrast to the distance and dialectic characterizing the sermons to seminarians, the more didactic tone of the congregational sermons, and the relative solemnity of the talks at ritual occasions.

Only a handful of the sermons had any title when they were delivered, so many of the titles here attached were added when I prepared the manuscript.

MONASTIC HOMILIES

THE POVERTY OF JESUS[1]

Luke 6:20–23

My brothers and sisters in Christ, when Jesus says that it is blessed to be poor, he does not suggest it as something extra for disciples. He is saying that every believer's life must somehow be characterized by poverty. It is not an option. Poverty is at the heart of following Jesus, of living within his kingdom.

This is a genuinely hard saying. So hard, that theologians have spent many years and many words discussing what it might mean. Much interesting discussion, to be sure, but missing the point. Jesus' declaration is not a theory to analyze but a challenge demanding a response. Because this is so difficult to face, we discuss and define and talk away the challenge into abstraction.

But if we accept it as a challenge, it is still a hard saying, in fact much harder. This has always been a difficult challenge, perhaps never so much as today. How can we be poor in a Christian way living in a society such as ours?

Some of us might ask, in fact, how we can afford to be poor. It is difficult enough, we think, just keeping the kids in shoes. Talk about poverty as a religious value seems an expensive luxury. When all the world is buying and selling as it has never bought and sold before, when keeping one's financial affairs in some sort of order demands almost constant attention, poverty seems personally a threat to be avoided rather than a value to be embraced.

Plus, poverty as we see it existing around us and within us seems only negative. It is the inability to do; it is care and hardship and trouble; it is powerlessness; it is alienation from others and disenfranchisement in the

---

1. To the monastic community and retreatants at Saint Joseph Abbey, Saint Benedict, Louisiana, June 7, 1969.

human city. We have indeed as a nation—with whatever ambiguous motives and with whatever ambiguous results—declared "war on poverty."

But still, Jesus says, to be blessed we must be poor.

If we want to discover what poverty might mean in our Christian lives today—in lives that seem so complex, that are involved and implicated in needs and anxieties of our own creation, that are unavoidably wealthy simply by existing in this grotesquely affluent country—if we really want to see what our Christian poverty might be, we must turn to the person of our Lord Jesus to study the model of true humanity. The poverty of Jesus is the pattern for our poverty.

The imitation of Jesus does not mean simplistically to shape our lives according to the economic structures of first-century Palestine. We live in our own time and within our own specific society. It is romantic fantasy to seek escape in some other one, even if that escape looks like the time and place when Jesus lived. Imitating Jesus' poverty does not demand that we be economically radical—that we go barefoot or live off the soil. It does require that we adhere within our own existence to the inner significance of Jesus' radical faith before God and his radical service to other humans.

It is true that Jesus was economically poor, in the sense that he was an itinerant preacher with no fixed residence and that he depended on the generosity of others to meet even his basic needs. But in these things, he was not entirely different from others among his contemporaries. It is not, in short, Jesus' sociological situation that serves as our model for poverty, but his religious response within that situation.

As we read the Gospel narratives, we see that what characterized Jesus' life was his absolute availability. The human Jesus was, first of all, completely at the disposition of his Father's will. Because he was obedient, he was poor. If by obedience we mean a deep and responsive hearing of another, a hearing that moves us out of self-preoccupation to the space and concern of another, then poverty is the necessary concomitant to obedience. To respond to the call of another—especially when that Other's call is sometimes difficult to discern—requires the emptying out of our own wishes, preconceptions, plans. And when this call is absolute, then the self-emptying is absolute; there is no limit placed on the response demanded by the call. Jesus came not to do his own will but that of the Father. Because he was absolutely at his Father's disposition, Jesus was poor. He was emptied of all that blocked the communication of love between himself and the Father.

When we follow the Gospel narratives closely, we see that Jesus' response to the Father's will was mediated—as it always is for us—by the needs of other people. Because he was the revelation of the Father's love for humans, Jesus was also at the absolute disposition of his brothers and sisters, to serve them, to be always accessible to their needs. Jesus' life was programmed, was shaped, only by his mission from the Father and by the needs of his brothers and sisters—precisely at the point where these two met.

When he would have slept, he was called to prayer; when he would have prayed, he was called to work; when he would have eaten, he was called to cure; when he wanted solitude, he was surrounded by crowds. Finally, when he wanted to live, when he begged that the cup of suffering be taken from him, he was called to the cross.

Because Jesus was obedient to the Father in every circumstance of his life, he was poor. Because Jesus was at the disposition of his brothers and sisters in every circumstance of his life, he was poor.

It is such poverty he declares as blessed. It is such poverty that we also can enact in all the circumstances of our lives. It is this poverty that makes us sharers in God's kingdom, and this poverty which brings the good news of God's kingdom to the world.

GOD'S SPIRIT[1]

Acts of the Apostles 11:1–17
Luke 9:45–49

My brothers in Christ, we have heard these words today from the Acts of the Apostles: "They were silenced, then praised God, saying, 'It is evident that the gift of repentance to life has been granted as well to the pagans.'"

The Spirit of God consistently shows himself greater than anything we can imagine. To draw us into all truth concerning Jesus, the Spirit must draw us out of the many private truths we have constructed for ourselves.

The range of the Holy Spirit's activity in the earliest church was far wider than Peter's Jewish preconceptions allowed for. The range of his activity in the world today is wider than our churchly preconceptions.

Just as Peter has to be brought to realize that God's gift extended even to the gentiles, so we too must constantly reflect on the fact that God's gift is wider and greater even now than any of our articulations of it.

What we possess in the church is the interior realization and the exterior articulation of God's mysterious gift of life. But just as that gift was given perfect expression in Jesus, our Lord, so is it always and everywhere offered to all people. Our mission, then, is not one of smug self-affirmation, but of humble thanksgiving. We seek here to give tongue in our songs and in our lives to the praise of God that is implicit and mute in the lives of all who are graced.

And because the Spirit that empowers the church is the Spirit of Jesus himself, we learn from the Gospel reading something else about the smallness, the humbleness of the way we make to the Father in the church.

---

1. To the monastic community at Saint Joseph Abbey, Saint Benedict, Louisiana, June 17, 1969.

We learn that neither the church nor any Christian individually can ever call down fire on anyone, can never seek to exclude or destroy, in the name of Jesus.

There is, to be sure, right and wrong. We may be right, and they may be wrong, as the Samaritans were wrong to refuse to accept Jesus. But we can never, possessing the Spirit of Jesus, force or coerce anyone into total orthodoxy, or sound opinion, or good practice. With Jesus, we can show the truth of God only by steadfastly facing Jerusalem, which way lies suffering and death. But which way also lies glory.

We are not, in short, our own measure. We possess, or better, are possessed by, the Spirit of Jesus, and he is the measure of our lives. The impulses of our hearts do not suffice, for God is greater than our hearts.

Like the Jewish believers in Acts, God will also reduce us to silence, but only so that we can then rise to praise the glory of his name, which is always and everywhere blessed through his Son.

THE PRICE OF PROPHECY[1]

Luke 3:1–18

My brothers in Christ, John the Baptizer is an endlessly fascinating figure. Especially fascinating, especially appealing to us at this historical moment—we who seek so desperately for, pray so urgently for, the voice of prophecy in the church. John, we think, is the kind of man we need in the church today, when in the wake of the great council so much is confused and conflicted.

At first glance, John seems in Luke's depiction of him all of one piece. He possesses a stunning simplicity and clarity, as bright and terrible as the desert he inhabits. He sees evil in the world: corruption in high places, graft and greed in the military, pride and smugness among religious leaders.

To all of this, John speaks a clear, unequivocal, and unyielding no. By his words and by his whole manner of life, he challenged the pervading falseness of the accepted order. And around this naysayer, there gathered disciples, there formed a movement. John was a power to be feared, but also a power that attracted. In the no of this baptizer there was no ambiguity, no compromise. He draws the lines that divide, cleanly and sharply.

And in this posture, we recognize in John the greatest born of woman, a man of heroic, almost Promethean, defiance. His very angularity, his very rigidity in the face of evil, his awful clarity seem to us to be a great thing and truly prophetic.

But if we gaze at John a bit longer, we see that the prophet's simplicity and singularity is deceiving, for his full significance lies not in his no but in his yes. John stands and points to another, whom he declares greater than himself. John's greatness lies not in his no, but in that yes. He says yes to Jesus, in whom he obscurely discerns the final yes of God to humans. This is John's final prophecy and his greatest.

1. Saint Meinrad Archabbey, St. Meinrad, Indiana, June 24, 1969.

In John's yes to Jesus, we learn how easy and natural is the prophetic no and how painfully hard the prophetic yes, because it is from his yes to Jesus that all of the ambiguity of his own life arose.

This man he baptized (who insisted that he be baptized) did not at all look like the Messiah John had expected, had announced, the "stronger One" with a winnowing fan to separate wheat and chaff, with an axe to lay to the roots. This Jesus does not take charge, but defers to the baptizer in meekness and obedience. So, John could not be sure.

John gladly went to prison because of his no to Herod's sin, for that was clear. But in prison, he suffered doubts and hesitations about his yes to Jesus. Wavering in his yes, he sent his followers to Jesus, and John died alone. His no to Herod brought his death, his yes to Jesus left him alone, no longer the head of a movement that could reshape society but only a solitary witness.

Like Jeremiah before him, John was a prophet commissioned to tear down, overthrow, and uproot. That was the easy part. But he was also to plant and to build. In this commission, he experienced, as do we all, the relative ease and certainty accompanying naysaying the evils and inadequacies so manifestly among us. And he experienced, as do we all, the difficulty and doubt that come with groping toward, pointing toward, the yes that will save us.

But John did point. He did say yes. And in his lonely death John was conformed to the death of him whom he announced, who is the yes of the Father to all his promises.

In this is John's true prophetic greatness. He shows us today that prophecy in the church can only be validated if it points to Jesus and leads to the truth concerning Jesus. He shows that as necessary as naysaying is, it gains its authentic worth only with reference to yea-saying, to affirmation. John shows that the final word of prophecy must be the willingness to die in obscurity for the sake of him who is greater than all prophecy, who is the word of love sent from God. To whom be praise forever.

HEALING AND SALVATION[1]

Luke 17:11–19

My brothers and sisters in Christ, whatever physical disfigurement the Jews called leprosy, it was a terrible affliction for those who had it. Their houses were destroyed, they were separated from their families, they were forced to leave town, they were declared unfit to worship with the community, they were forbidden contact with the healthy. They had to live on the outskirts of society in the company of others so designated by religious authorities.

A more complete state of estrangement, of alienation, could hardly be imagined. And given the state of medical practice in antiquity, there was no hope for a cure at the hands of doctors. Those declared leprous faced a living death, an existence stripped of everything that made human existence meaningful: home, family, community, even worship. Theirs was a desperate condition.

The reading from the Gospel of Luke we have just read introduces us to ten such leprous men and their encounter with Jesus, who is on his way to Jerusalem to face his own death. They may have heard of him as a traveling wonderworker, and as men beyond despair, they had nothing to lose by appealing to him as he passed by. They hail him from a distance and with respect: "Jesus . . . Master." And then, "Have pity on us." People in such a pitiable condition asking for pity seek more than pity. They seek help. They seek healing. Perhaps this wonderworker can do something.

Jesus gazes at them. He says, "Go, show yourselves to the priests." Jewish priests were in charge of this sort of thing. They were the ones assigned by the law to judge whether an individual had the affliction or not, whether

---

1. To the monastic community and lay congregation at Saint Joseph Abbey, Saint Benedict, Louisiana, August 24, 1969.

he was fit to return to society and worship or not. The priests could not make people free of leprosy; they could only declare them free of leprosy.

At Jesus' command, all ten lepers start off. They are not sure why they should show themselves to the priests, since they were all obviously still leprous. But they were desperate and willing to do as this stranger told them. Perhaps they trusted his authoritative tone. Maybe they thought something might, after all, happen.

And something does. Before they ever get to the priests, they discover that they are cleansed of their leprosy. They are healed. The story does not in fact tell us whether nine of them continued on to receive priestly scrutiny or not. Probably they did, eager, as is natural, to be restored to family, society, and worship, and needing the priests' OK for such a return. They forgot, as is natural, Jesus. Only one of them returned to thank Jesus with all his heart. And it is only this one that Jesus declares not only healed but saved, because of his faith.

Let us consider this just for a moment.

Ten men in an absolutely helpless condition ask Jesus for help. He gives them an order. Before they can fulfill it, they are changed, they are cured. All of them. Now here is the curious thing: nine of them carry out the directive, then go home, never thinking of Jesus again. Why?

Perhaps because their trust in him was only the sort of trust that people put in a dispenser of medicines: follow the prescription and all will be well. You never have to think about the doctor again. Carrying out the order is sufficient. What to do is all that counts. The nine remembered the order, all right, and forgot the one who gave the order.

But the cure, Luke tells us, happened before any of them had the chance to actually carry out that command. They must all have realized that. They must all have realized that the cure could not have come from fulfilling the command, but it could only have come from this stranger whom they had hailed on the road and asked for pity.

But only one acted on that realization. Only one recognized that the order and its fulfillment was not the point so much as was recognizing the one who issued the order and whose power healed them. This man's response was not to the directive but to Jesus. He returned, and gave thanks, and was declared not only healed, but saved, because of his faith.

Faith, we learn, is more than crying out for help when desperate; faith is more than carrying out a command. Faith is answering yes to the one who calls us. It is saying "thank you" to the one who heals us. Faith cannot stop at the confession of belief, cannot pause at the doing of good works, but must extend into thanksgiving—must reach through to the amen spoken through all our lives in thanks to the One who has healed us.

My sisters and brothers, our alienation has been no less acute, our sickness no less real than that of the ten lepers. And in our distress, we have called on the name of Jesus. We have received healing from the command of the One on whom we have called. So we too must return, as we have today at this Eucharist, to express our faith in thanksgiving to him who saves us.

THE ENGINE OF HYPOCRISY[1]

Hebrews 10:26–31
Luke 12:1–8

My brothers in Christ, Jesus tells his followers—and us—to beware the leaven of the Pharisees that is hypocrisy. But we, so we would like to think, are the last people needing that warning. Hypocrisy is universally scorned among us. Translated as phoniness or inauthenticity, hypocrisy is our favorite target for contempt. Hypocrisy is the vice we most like to discover in those with whom we disagree, and the one we consider least likely to be discovered among those with whom we agree.

But hypocrisy is a very subtle vice, much subtler than the risible antics of a Uriah Heep or the prayerful posturing of religious con artists. It is so subtle that it can thrive precisely within a carefully cultivated atmosphere of freedom and openness, of honesty and candor, of religious "transparency." It may even thrive among such right-thinking people as ourselves.

Hypocrisy is a vice of misplaced emphasis, a derangement of desire. It desires rather to appear to be than to be.

We who are quick to spot some traditional expressions of hypocrisy in the exposed lies of politicians and prelates might do well to ask ourselves a hard question concerning hypocrisy: May it not be present in more subtle ways even in our desire to appear open and honest and candid and tolerant and forgiving, before we have actually undergone the grueling discipline necessary to become persons with these positive qualities?

The engine that drives hypocrisy—as also other forms of duplicity and dishonesty—is fear, specifically the fear of other people. Here is where hypocrisy has grasped a great truth but has misplaced the emphasis. The truth is that as humans we truly are under judgment, and judgment is to be feared. The misplaced emphasis is shifting such judgment from the gaze

1. Saint Meinrad Archabbey, St. Meinrad, Indiana, September 11, 1969.

13

of God to the gaze of other finite creatures. The poor and partial opinions of other people concerning our worth—our acceptability in their eyes—replace the judgment of God, which alone can truly weigh our worth and declare us acceptable.

The hypocrite is one who lives in fear of the judgment rendered by other people, and so pretends to be something he is not. Let's be quite honest. We are all prey to such fear. Peer pressure, role expectations, social standards, organizational demands—these are all real; they stand in daily judgment on us. In one way or another, they test our adequacy, our acceptability. Yes. They do.

The question, though, is whether we consider such judgments to be ultimate, or act as though they actually determined our human value. Does our life gain its final validity from the judgment rendered by people as finite and partial in their perceptions as we are? Do we then become, out of our fear of such judgment, slaves to human opinion, so that we act in ways that do not correspond to the truth discerned by God in our hearts?

In Matthew 10:28, Jesus tells his followers—and us—not to fear those who can destroy the body, but to fear the One who can destroy both body and soul in hell. Jesus places the emphasis in the right place. Judgment is a reality, and the judgment of God is more scathing and harrowing than any that can be imagined by humans. It is more penetrating and intimate than the trivial opinions connected to social convention, political ideologies, and the fashions of the age. This judgment is rendered at every moment by the Power that has called us into existence and that alone sustains us in our existence (even now!) and to which our existence has its only ultimate reference. This judgment poses a question to our entire existence, and the One who poses that question, it is him we must fear. As the Letter to the Hebrews declares in our reading today, "It is a terrifying thing to fall into the hands of the living God" (Heb 10:31).

But what is the character of this fear? It is not the engine that makes us into craven cowards in the sight of others. This fear of God is an *absolute* fear; it is the richly ambivalent combination of awe and dread and respect and, yes, fascination, and, yes, love, with which we stand beneath and face the ultimate, the truth that lies far beyond every human gaze and opinion.

And here is the paradox: this absolute fear liberates us from our desire to please every human opinion, meet every human expectation—and fake it if we must. It liberates us to live in authentic existence before and with other humans. Just as the love of God reveals to us the relativity and indeed the idolatry of our many human loves, so does this deep and responsive awe before the questioning presence of God free us from our enslavement to human judgment. We have only One to whom we must ultimately answer, and he knows who we are already; from his gaze there is no escape, in his eyes no pretense is possible.

We are free, then, to exist authentically. We answer not to the whims of others, or even our own whims. We answer yes faithfully to the loving power that places us in existence, and yes lovingly to all other humans. It is even possible for us to stand in witness to him who for us first answered yes with the perfect yes to the Father, Jesus the Lord. And we can hope, even in the darkness of our many fears (and, yes, they do remain), that he whom we confess as Lord may also accept us as brothers.

JUST DO IT[1]

Matthew 5:21–26
James 2:8–13

My brothers in Christ, the Scriptures do not make very good escape reading. They have a disturbing way of calling our attention again and again in simple words to a few simple truths. For the number of important truths is not really so large. It is not difficult to learn them. What is difficult is doing them. This is because the important truths are not theories or mathematical formulae we can know with the head alone. They are the truths of God, and they can only really be known in the doing of them, in love.

Thus, in the Gospel of Matthew, Jesus does not clarify whether this brother of ours who has something against us is in the right or the wrong. That question of legality could be discussed endlessly: Who stepped on whose toes first, and who is to blame? We could spend the rest of our lives spinning lucid rationalizations on how justified we are in not speaking to our brother. He hit me first. I am the victim here. But Jesus cuts through the tangle of self-righteousness and says: It doesn't matter who is right and who is wrong. Your job is to be reconciled. Ask forgiveness, or extend forgiveness—the word means "letting go"—and either become at peace with your brother, or do not bother trying to make peace with me.

Thus also, in the Letter of James, we are told that if we have started showing preferences in whom we love, we have already missed the point. We have already confused the love of God revealed to us in the death of Jesus with the kind of love that is merely poetical. The law of love, that law which liberates, says James, is just as stringent as the old law. It is in fact even more stringent, for the demands of authentic liberty are harrowing. There is no point at which we can say "enough." There is no goal at which

1. Saint Meinrad Archabbey, St. Meinrad, Indiana, September 20, 1969.

we can say "finished." There is no class of humans, no range of request, that we can close off and say that the law does not apply. There is no end to becoming a Christian.

The truths we must learn are really very few. In the end there is actually only one truth, which is the love of God revealed to us in the man who went to all lengths of love, who went to his death for love, in order to reconcile us . . . who did not deserve it. This is the only truth we need learn. But we only get to know it by doing it.

GOD AND CAESAR[1]

Matthew 22:15–22

My brothers in Christ, one of the more subtle and constant tempta-
tions of Christians, and certainly Christian preachers, is to reduce
the significance of the gospel to the merely private. It is understandable.
Matters of the heart are complex enough. But when we set about to apply
the gospel to the world around us, we are quickly overwhelmed.

Engagement with the world inevitably involves engagement with
politics, and politics is notoriously messy. If only we had some clarity, some
consistent measure.

The Pharisees who question Jesus in today's reading had a certain form
of clarity, a certain kind of measure. They attached the banner of religion to
a particular political stance. All the good things belong to this faction, all
the bad people to that. A wonderfully neat scheme that—it would seem—
enables one to judge the worth of a religious message by the standard of
the political, and the quality of the political message by the standard of the
religious. A Manichaean dream.

It is just this sort of pairing off, though, that Jesus refuses. He says,
"Pay to Caesar what is Caesar's and to God what is God's." This seemingly
clever retort to a trick question is impressive; we are all proud of Jesus
being so witty in such a fraught setting. In reality, though, Jesus states a
truly frightening principle. He categorically separates the unholy alliance
between throne and altar. His disjunction does not make things easier, but
harder.

It still leaves us the task of judging every Caesar precisely as Caesar,
and not as a god or demon. It leaves us the task of judging every government precisely as government. We are forced to make sober and rational

1. Saint Meinrad Archabbey, St. Meinrad, Indiana, October 29, 1969.

18

decisions on the basis of realistic politics, often in areas that are covered by no moral law and seem remote from the concerns of religion.

Even harder, we are to render to God what is God's. God is not just another political alternative. But neither can we render to God totally abstracted from political allegiances and political programs. But God stands before us as the ultimate question put to all our allegiances, all our programs. Every political platform and every social initiative stands under the judgment of his word. All of which is to say, we are left free to engage the world as world, but our freedom in and for the world is responsible to its, and our, Creator.

We can abdicate the responsibility imposed by such freedom either by ideologizing the faith or by hermetically sealing the faith off from social reality.

Or, we can, in the fugitive joy of true freedom, walk with humility before God's face, making the difficult and obscure decisions we must make as humans with and for each other, aware and somehow glad that all such decisions must be and constantly are being held in judgment by the word of God.

SCRIBES OF GOD'S KINGDOM[1]

Sirach 51:13–30
Matthew 13:45–53

My brothers in Christ, the scribe was an important religious figure in ancient Judaism. He was a professional interpreter of Scripture—the law, the prophets, the wisdom literature. But he was also a teacher of the people. Even more than the priest, the scribe mediated God's word to the people and instructed them in the ways of the Lord.

The scribe therefore was required to spend many hours in careful study—seeking out the true implications of the law, learning by heart the maxims of the sages, memorizing the words of the prophets.

But the goal of the scribe's study was not an abstract knowledge detached from real life. Because the subject he studied was the word of the living God, a word which was itself living and active, if he was authentically to learn it and authentically to teach it, he had himself to internalize it. He had to become that which he studied and about which he taught. The true scribe was not the one who had only memorized the law and prophets and could analyze the sayings of the wise. The true scribe was the one who lived the law, followed the prophets, and was himself among the wise.

Today's first reading from Sirach, thus, shows the young scribe at the beginning of his career. It does not describe the rigorous classroom training he must have gone through. We hear nothing of his academic standing. We hear instead of his overpowering thirst for the wisdom that was the substance and meaning of his life. He hungered, he worked for, he awaited and prayed for the gift of wisdom. Without that gift within him, the first element of which was fear of the Lord, no amount of memorization would be of any use.

---

1. To theology students at Saint Meinrad Archabbey, St. Meinrad, Indiana, November 22, 1969.

This is because for the teacher of religion, for the minister of God's word, the medium is, in the strictest sense, the message. If there is no personal appropriation of the truth in the life of the teacher/scribe, there is no message. The word becomes simply words—abstract, lifeless, cold. Wisdom can be communicated only through the wise, prophecy only by prophets, God's law only by those consumed by love of that law.

In chapter 13 of his Gospel, Matthew places the parables of Jesus in the context of wisdom teaching. The parables of Jesus are in fact a form of wisdom discourse. They are riddles put to our existence and challenge that existence. And here, at the end of his parable-discourse, Jesus speaks of the scribes of God's kingdom. Do they grasp the parables? Do they hear their challenge? Jesus speaks to his immediate disciples who will, after his resurrection, teach to all nations all that he commanded. He speaks equally, however, to those preparing to be ministers of the gospel. We are to be the scribes of the kingdom of heaven.

The parables of Jesus form the wisdom sayings of the new covenant. They are the subject of our study as scribes of that covenant. But they remain only a set of clever analogies, both for us and for those we teach, unless we take the parables into our hearts as personal challenges.

Unless we ourselves have allowed ourselves to be challenged by the parable's call to conversion, unless we ourselves have seen the kingdom of God as a pearl of great price or as a treasure hidden in a field and have sold all to purchase it; unless we have taken the risk of staking all we are and have on this kingdom; unless and until we have done this, the gospel will remain for us—and for all whom we teach—a school exercise, something to be memorized and learned by rote. It will remain irrelevant to those we teach because it is irrelevant to us.

Unless we have faced the demand of these parables to change our whole outlook on life in view of the reality of God in Christ Jesus, we are playing games, and our study hours, and our liturgy, and our quest for community is empty.

All of us together, and each one of us individually in the secrecy of the heart, acknowledge the truth that unless we repent and believe the gospel, we will not be the scribes of the kingdom of heaven who bring out new things as well as old, but will be pretenders who draw out of the storehouse of our inadequacy the boring staleness of our own sinful condition.

HEARING GOD'S WORD[1]

Romans 2:17–24
Luke 8:4–21

Nothing is more central to our self-understanding as Christians than that we are a people that hears the word of God. It is a conviction everywhere expressed and approved by Scripture. Jesus tells us by parable that those who hear the word will bear fruit (Luke 8:15) and says directly, "My mother and brothers are those who hear the word of God and keep it" (8:21). And when a woman from the crowd praises his mother, Jesus retorts, "Rather, blessed are those who hear the word of God and keep it" (8:27–28).

Paul too declares that faith comes from hearing (Gal 3:5). He praises the Thessalonians for receiving his preaching "for what it really is, the word of God" (1 Thess 2:13). In another place, he asks, "How can they believe if they have not heard?" (Rom 10:14). Hearing the word is essential to the response of faith: when Abraham heard God, Paul tells us, "He believed, and it was reckoned to him as righteousness" (Rom 4:3; Gen 15:6).

So familiar is this conviction that it can easily become a cliché. Clichés, as we know, are truths that with frequent repetition and ill-frequent examination are halfway to becoming mere slogans.

Clichés do contain an element of truth. That's another cliché! The problem is that the cliché's element of truth may no longer be our truth even as we repeat it. In fact, the cliché can be a barrier between us and the truth it seeks to express. Does my bumper sticker proclaim that I would rather split wood than atoms? Then I may consider myself a peacemaker and nonpolluter even as, puffing on a cigarette, I violently curse my way through a traffic jam.

---

1. Saint Joseph Abbey, Saint Benedict, Louisiana, December 1969.

The attractiveness of clichés is undeniable. Most of us, indeed, prefer living with them. Too much examination is exhausting. Let's live with simplified slogans. Easier to declare "Better Dead than Red" than figure out the difference between Soviet and Yugoslavian communism.[2] Because clichés simplify the complexities of real life, they enable us to act. They free us from the burden of thought, so we can get things done. Advertising slogans work so well, after all, because they give us a packaged truth that motivates us to buy a packaged product.

I worry that even the truth that we are a people that hears the word of God can become a cliché and therefore a distortion of truth that is proclaimed more than lived. One way this happens is if we suppose that "God's word" is something easily identifiable and available to us, like a safe-deposit box in the bank. Examples? We objectify God's word and make it our possession when we absolutely identify it with the texts of the Bible, or the doctrines of the church, or even the customs of this religious community.

When we do this, we forget that God has not ceased speaking, that he is not a dead God who can be boxed but a living God who escapes our grasp and control. His word is not simply memorialized in texts from the past but alive and active in new and surprising ways every day. God's word is not our safe possession that we need no longer hear because we already know what it says. It is a dangerous threat that breaks the boundaries of our compulsive need to control and demands that we pay attention. God's word is not our safe possession.

Another way the truth becomes a cliché is when we conclude that since we hear God's word, no one else does. Paul was outraged when his fellow Jews had this attitude about Torah: "Is He the God of the Jews only? Is He not the God of the Gentiles also? Yes, of the Gentiles also, since God is one" (Rom 3:29). With this attitude, we think we do not need to pay attention to the religious claims or life experiences of others, for how could God be at work among them? Very subtly, God's word again becomes a possession we own, a means by which we assert our worth at the expense of others. We display the kind of arrogance Paul chastises among those who had Torah: "You are sure that you are a guide to the blind, a light to those who are in darkness, a corrector of the foolish, a teacher of children, having in Torah the embodiment of knowledge and truth—you, then, who teach others, will you not teach yourselves?" (Rom 2:19–20).

2. The references disclose the historical period.

It is easy to applaud Paul's attack on his fellow Jews, but harder to accept that many of us Christians act in the same way: "We don't need to listen to anything or anyone else. We have nothing to learn. We have God's word." This disposition carries with it a great sense of certainty, for it closes off any possible complexity or ambiguity. But is such certainty the result of attentiveness to God's word or the effect of systemic deafness?

The hearing of God's word can become a cliché also by overextension, which can happen in two ways.

First, we can easily elide the word we hear and the words that we speak. God's word is made to stretch amazingly to sanctify the projects we fashion and the politics we espouse. God's word embraces political platforms and zoning ordinances.

Second, we can assume that since we hear God's word, then it follows that we also obey, observe, and act according to God's word, so that we can carry about with us an air of moral and religious superiority.

Such distortions have in common the turning of God's word into a human possession—rather than a gift from Another, it is something we can own and cling to—and, as our possession, it serves to enhance our own worth, rather than to point toward the presence of God in the world, becomes a means of our glory rather than God's glory.

How can we break out of our self-constructed cliché and rediscover the truth within it so that it might again become a living truth for us?

A good start is giving up the pretense of possession. Remember again that the word is not our own but the word of the One whom we do not control but who controls us, who moves ahead of us in dark and mysterious fashion, and in whose sight every human pretense is laid bare and reduced to nothingness.

It is good for us, therefore, to have some modesty when speaking of God's word. And this is not as difficult to achieve as might be supposed. All we need do is ask: What is it that we really mean when we say we hear God's word? What is it and where is it? We quickly discover that "God's word" is not so clear and obvious and irrefutable as we assumed; it is, rather, slippery, elusive, and deeply ambiguous.

Is the word of God found in Scripture? We resoundingly respond, "Yes!" But if we ask, "How are those fragmentary texts from long ago and far away God's word and not simply the historical record of merely human words?," we become less cocky. What is it about the words of Peter and Paul and Mark and John that commands our assent that through them God speaks to us today? And if we seek in their words a clear and compelling and absolutely consistent directive for any aspect of our lives beyond the obvious, we quickly grow discouraged by the inconsistency, incoherence, and even contradictions these texts contain. Scripture is indeed the word of God. But how? Scripture is the norm for our lives, but the multitude of interpretations of that norm, even by learned and saintly believers, is sufficiently diverse as to give us pause.

Is the word of God heard also through creation, in the contours of God's crafting, with their multiform patterns of beauty and order? Does creation express by its song the power of the cosmic lyricist? We say, "Yes!" Yet that assent is made more cautiously when nature's fang and claw slash too close to home, and when our neighbors see chaos where we perceive order, confusion where we detect a pattern, caprice where we discern purpose, cruel chance where we apprehend gentle providence. Do we and our neighbors dwell in different worlds? Is God's word expressed clearly in nature or not?

But since this is the word of the living God, we must hear it spoken in the narratives of human lives, our own stories and those of others. In our sorrows and joys, fears and fragile hope, in the collapse of fantasy and the construction of love, in the words of care and compassion that pass between us, surely we hear the word of God whispered through the body language of our life together. "Yes," we say, again.

Yet, how hard to discern, how difficult to detect, the work and word of God in our lives. When is my experience—our experience—so lucid, its consequences so plain, that I can boldly declare, here, indeed, God is at work? Perhaps for you such a hearing of God's word is frequent and easy. For me, not.

So, we have good reasons for modesty. All of us confess that the word of God is spoken to us in Scripture, in the world around us, in our shared lives. Yet, none of us can demonstrate with clarity or sufficient power even to convince ourselves what that word actually is.

Precisely here, I think, is the chance to discover the truth within the cliché. We ask: Is God's word really something *out there* in text or world or experience in an objective form, able to be discerned by all in the way planes are spotted by radar? Or is it the case that the act of human hearing is itself at least partially constitutive of God's word?

Does creation, for example, speak the glory of God to all or only to those who listen to the rain and hail and summer breeze for the voice of the

Creator? Do the human experiences of alienation and love become articulate with God's presence for all or only for those who attend in life's dark passages to the echo of Another's voice? Do the Scriptures shape the lives of all who read them or only those who place themselves humbly before them as the wisdom that comes from God and who discover in them God's word?

This is, in truth, a frightening proposal. If God's word is not something "out there" that we might possess, but is rather something we must evoke out of silence by the quality of our hearing, then we must look even more closely at how we listen.

How can we hear God's word in the world, in our lives, and in the texts of Scripture, when we have for so long neglected the simple discipline of listening at all? We cannot hear the song of bird or whisper of dragonfly if our ears are assaulted by noise. We cannot hear the texts of Scripture without the silence that makes us receptive to what is other. We cannot hear the plea and prayer of our neighbors if we refuse to stifle the inner monologue of our self-preoccupation.

If we walk through our world with a stereo stuck in our ears, we cannot hear that word. If we walk through our lives with slogans between our ears, we do not hear the cries of others. If we walk through the Bible with smugness covering our ears, we do not hear its message.

Clichés that lose all touch with reality are called lies.

SERMONS FOR SEMINARIANS

FEAR AND FAITH[1]

Luke 12:22–31

My brothers and sisters in Christ, in this passage from the Gospel of Luke, we learn something about ourselves and something about our God.

What we learn about ourselves is important, naturally—it is us, after all! More important, though, is that it is God who is telling us about ourselves. What we learn about him, then, is that he knows us very well indeed. This is a scary proposition.

We learn that God has known all along that we are creatures filled with fear, has known all along that most of what we do in our lives is driven by and shadowed by fear.

We are anxious about our lives, true, what we shall eat, and about our bodies, true, what we shall wear. But our fear is more ingenious and adapts itself to every circumstance. We fear failure: What will I do if I fail this test? Will I pass? Get high pass? Cover myself in honors?[2] Perversely, we fear success as much as failure. What if I do well in this test, in this paper, in this sermon, what then? What great expectations will I stir up in others, and in myself—will I have to top my performance every time?

We fear discovery. Someone, sometime, somewhere, will find out how little I really know, how little I really am. I will be found naked on the bus ... show up late ... lose my notes ... forget my lines ... and awake in terror from those anxiety dreams that somehow speak the truth about our lives.

We fear being afraid, fear others will suspect how very much we are afraid.

---

1. Marquand Chapel, Yale Divinity School, New Haven, Connecticut, November 14, 1977.
2. The YDS grading system then was pass, high pass, honors; few, if any, failed.

How terribly efficient is this cold secret we hold to ourselves, knot tightly around our hearts. What a wealth of phantoms it conjures in the corners of our mind. And what a perfect motor, this fear, driving us to measure cubits if we cannot add them, driving us to gather whatever small sticks we can, the small kindling of possessions and achievement, of success and esteem, to build for ourselves a small fire, just a small fire, against the chill of the fear of death.

"Yes," God says, almost yawning, "I know all this about you. Yes," says God, almost smiling, "I have known it all along. I know it is fear that drives you to seek after all these things. I know that you need them, these proofs that you exist, have worth, are something after all. I marvel at your energy, I admire your little motor, but I suspect that you grow weary, having to construct all this every day by yourself. And really, all the people in all the nations do this sort of thing, don't they? All people everywhere. Haven't you learned something by being my special people that might make you different?"

So, we stop short, and say to God: "You really know this about me? You really already know how hard it is for me to rise and face the terrors of my day, how difficult to stand and to speak, how frightened I am that someone in this room will discover that I am naked? Can you really see through all the walls and moats and strong battlements I have so carefully constructed, and can you really peer into this dark empty chamber where the cold motor runs night and day? You are a God who knows all this, and you are not appalled? You know the secret of my fear and do not turn away? I am puzzled."

And we imagine God saying, "Appalled? No. A little disappointed, maybe. You have maybe allowed yourself to get so locked in your fear that you forget what it is to have a God like me, a God who speaks to you, who comes to you, and says, 'Do not fear, do not be anxious.' Now, really, if I tell you not to fear, if I tell you that all is well, why don't you believe it, you people of little trust? What better authority do you require?"

In this fashion, Jesus speaks to us today in this gathering, not out of the distant past, when he too tasted fear and shuddered at the unbearable terror of death, but today, in the powerful presence of his Holy Spirit, and he tells us, "Put first things first. Seek the kingdom of God, and these things will be yours as well."

And out of our great, our incessant fear, we cry out, "Aha, another task to perform, another way to prove ourselves. We must seek, strive, go on a trek, do things for the kingdom!" And our fear revs its great motor, and great clouds of spiritual exhaust trail after us as we hurry on that quest.

But there is a still-further word from Jesus. He says, "Do not fear, little flock"—such graciousness in the language of our God—"it is your Father's good pleasure"—he is our Father, this dark mystery we fear above all, and he takes pleasure in being our Father—it is his pleasure, Jesus tells us, "to give you the kingdom."

So, then, it is a gift? Yes, a gift. And already given.

Because I have this gift from the One I most fear, the gift first of all of being known absolutely in my fear, and then being told by him it is all right, "do not be afraid"—it is because of this gift that I need not cling to all the tattered rags of possessions and human reputation. I can even, in fact, share this gift. I can, indeed, give away what I have in money and time and energy and care to those whom, I suspect, have all along been as fearful as me—perhaps even fearful of me—but who have not had, perhaps, anyone to say to them "Do not be afraid."

But my fear says, more softly, "How do I know that you have given me the kingdom?"

And my fear hears, finally, "Am I not speaking to you today?"

RESURRECTION BODIES[1]

Acts of the Apostles 4:8–12
Luke 24:36–49

My sisters and brothers in Christ, I am troubled by all this talk about bodies in the passages we have heard. If the disciples were wrong when they thought Jesus was just a spirit, then so am I. A spirit, Jesus tells the disciples (and me), does not have these hands and feet, flesh and bones.

They were staggered, and—in a puzzling phrase—"did not believe for joy." So Jesus, keeping a straight face, asks, "Do you have something here to eat?"

Why do I find this disturbing? Why do I secretly wish Loisy to be right and Tertullian wrong?[2] Why do I want more of spirit here, more of "resurrected faith" and less of flesh?

Is it because if Jesus were resurrected only as spirit and not as spiritual body, I could hold him in my head with the Pythagorean theorem and the second law of thermodynamics and the Chalcedonian formula[3]—available and applicable, and at my bidding?

But if he is a body, then I might bump into him anywhere, perhaps in a cripple at the church door, or a wino in Grand Central Station, or the bag lady on the Green,[4] who asks, with a straight face, "Do you have something here to eat?"

---

1. Marquand Chapel, Yale Divinity School, New Haven, Connecticut, April 29, 1982.

2. Alfred Loisy declared that "faith rose on Easter." Tertullian famously defended the bodily resurrection, as in *De Carne Christi*.

3. The Council of Chalcedon in 451 defined Christ in ontological terms as "two natures in one person."

4. I was commuting weekly by train to Manhattan to teach and had time to study Grand Central Station's denizens; the Green is the downtown New Haven Green, where the homeless gathered.

I cannot control this Jesus so well as the One who rises spiritually by my resurrection faith, the One who adds interest to my private drama to the degree that I can suspend disbelief, willingly, and agree to pretend "as if."

If Jesus can bump into me on the street, if I might see him this afternoon on Whalley Avenue, then he is really alive. He is real. I must take him into account.

How frightening if the resurrection is not a dogma but a fact, not a fantasy but as real and ordinary as potatoes.

If I were one of the disciples in this story, I don't know if I'd want my mind opened to the Scripture if it meant I had to watch out for Jesus on every street corner or random porch.[5] I'd start to get worried as soon as I heard he was not just a spirit. I'd think, "Uh-oh, now I can't just carry the thought of him in my head or decode him from the text of the Bible; now I'm going to have to decipher that puzzled posture down the hall, that dragging foot on the stairs, that smile cracking carefully along the edges. I'll have to look a little harder at the shape of things and how they speak."

Worse still, I shall have to attend to my own body, which I resent. Hard enough, anyway, to figure out where it starts and where it ends, my body, what is spirit and what is not. But if Jesus' body tells me of my own future, then I must consider more closely my alliances and entanglements. If the way I dispose of my body signals the disposition of my spirit, I cannot any longer say "food for the belly, the belly for food," when the body is for the Lord.

All this attentiveness spells weariness and pain. Thinking thoughts is clean and easy. Thoughts stand still. Thinking bodies is messy and endless, changing constantly as they do. But if my body is my loudest and clearest word, then I cannot bear witness just by saying "Jesus is raised." I must reach out, as he did, and touch the body of the crippled man, and say, "In the name of Jesus, walk."

All this is so, of course, only if the Gospel is more than a story about the past of the disciples and is also about our present stories. And it is, we say, for the resurrected One lives with God's own life; and as God holds each of us out of nothingness at this moment freely in an excess of love, so is Jesus as close to us, closer to us, as we are to each other in this room, and can walk as easily through the doors of our fear as he did through their closed doors back then, can even, we hold, insinuate himself into casual loaves of bread.

5. An allusion to J. D. Salinger's *Franny and Zooey*: the "fat lady on the porch."

So there is not only trouble in these words about the body, there is also the grace of our Lord, Jesus Christ, whose body is not far distant from those who gather in his name, whose body is not alone a threat to our comfort but also a comfort to our anguish.

It is the Jesus who bodies forth in our bodies[6] and whose spirit leaps to life in our fellowship, who feeds us in this meal we share. Through him may all praise be given, in the Holy Spirit, to our gracious God.

6. The allusion is to Gerard Manley Hopkins, "Glory Be to God for Dappled Things."

PROPHECY AND IDOLATRY[1]

Amos 8:4–12

A good working definition of prophecy is speech that, no matter when it was spoken and heard, no matter when it was written or read, cuts to the heart of the human condition by exposing it to God's truth. By that definition—or, for that matter, any definition—Amos of Tekoa is the prophet's prophet.

These words from Amos we have heard read to us today were spoken and transcribed almost 3,000 years ago. Yet they are as precise in their dissection of the human heart in our age as they were in the age of the prophet. This is in part because, well, Amos is a prophet. But it is also in part because the patterns of idolatry do not change.

Idolatry is not a matter of incensing the wrong statue. It is a matter of disordered loyalties, of the derangement of the heart. It is a perennial disease of the human spirit.

Idolatry identifies being and worth with having. To have more is to be more. Idolatry expresses the logic of envy: if you have more than me, then you are more than me. And since there is only a limited amount of stuff to go around, the logic of envy is the logic of violence and murder: only when I eliminate the competition do I win.

Idolatry so understood serves the needy god of endless craving and desire. We hear its voice clearly in those Amos accuses of "trampling on the needy and bringing the poor of the land to ruin": they say, "We will make the ephah small and the shekel great"—this is called rigging the market; "we will practice deceit with false balances"—this is called creative bookkeeping; "we will buy the poor for silver and the needy for a pair of sandals"—this is called shrewd hiring practice; "we will sell the sweepings

---

1. Summer School at the Boston College Institute for Religious Education and Pastoral Ministry, Chestnut Hill, Massachusetts, July 1, 1994.

of the wheat"—this formerly was called watering the milk, and now it's planned obsolescence.

The voice we hear is not from long ago and far away. It is the voice we hear every day on radio and television and read every day in magazine ads and cereal boxes. It is, indeed, our national voice.

We are set to celebrate the birthday of the nation, Independence Day. What a sad decline, from the proclamation of liberty as the freedom to serve God according to conscience, to the celebration of liberty as release from every duty and responsibility except that of acquisition and exploitation.

Amos levels a threat against those ancient exploiters and murderers—we recall that Sirach says anyone who withholds the wages of the poor person has committed murder—a threat that is all the more frightening because it is self-fulfilling. God will send a famine on the land, Amos declares, "not a famine of bread or a thirst for water, but of hearing the words of the Lord."

Idolatry's final enslavement of us happens when the only voice we can hear is our own, and we are abandoned to the closed circuitry of craving, competition, and corruption.

In our age, in this land and decade, we see all around us those who, in Amos's words, "wander from sea to sea and from north to east; they run to and fro, seeking the word of the Lord . . . and they do not find it." Perhaps we are among them, sad empty questers for spirituality, for self.

Certainly, we recognize the voice of idolatry as our voice as well. Maybe not in buying and selling. Perhaps not in exploitative labor practices. But in envy of each other's gifts; in competition for honor; in sadness at another's achievement; in rejoicing in another's failing; in craving the corner where the light falls and the room with the extra bookshelves; in longing, longing, longing . . . for the satisfaction of the self, that ever-thirsty, ever-hungry little god. We are infected by, and in turn spread our national disease through, the secret passageways and dark needlehouses of spiritual envy.

If we look only to ourselves, we have reason to despair, because by our own strength we cannot escape idolatry. It is our natural aptitude.

That is why we have gathered here, not to hear our own word but to hear God's word. For when we look not to ourselves but to God, we have hope. We remember that our life is not a possession to be made secure by acquisition and defense but a gift to be received at every moment from the One who, as James tells us, gives to all simply and without grudging. One such gift from the Father of lights is the voice of prophecy itself, which make us squirm because it knows us so well, but which also heals because it is true.

LAZARUS AND US[1]

Jeremiah 32:1–3
First Timothy 6:6–10, 17–19
Psalm 91
Luke 16:19–31

My sisters and brothers in Christ, today's readings speak of a dimension of our embodiedness that Scripture takes far more seriously than sex, namely, the use of material possessions.

Scripture actually pays very little attention to sexual behavior. But it speaks constantly about the ways humans deal with the things God has created for their use and pleasure.

Here's one of the obvious ways in which we do not dwell in the world constructed by Scripture. We are more than willing to deduce from peoples' sexual arrangements the state of their soul. We hardly notice how their use of possessions is an even more profound symbol of their self-disposition.

For Scripture, the issue is not that we have possessions—so long as we are bodies, we cannot avoid possessing—or even so much what we possess—although circumstances might make that matter a great deal—but above all *how* we possess.

Does our possessing things work to serve God, as an expression of faith, or in service to possessions themselves, as an expression of idolatry? Jesus says as much in the passage immediately preceding the one we have read: "No servant," he says, "can serve two masters; either the servant will hate the one master and love the other, or will be devoted to one and despise the other. You cannot serve both God and Mammon" (Luke 6:13). It is on hearing this declaration, in fact, that Jesus' listeners, whom Luke calls "lovers of money," mock him (16:14), leading Jesus to respond with the parable of Lazarus and the rich man.

1. Cannon Chapel, Candler School of Theology, Atlanta, Georgia, ca. 2000.

"You cannot serve both God and Mammon." We notice that Jesus assumes that humans inevitably serve something as ultimate, and in this he agrees with all of Scripture. Our freedom is always aligned with something or someone we consider greater than us and whom we serve. But if we spend our lives serving what is not truly ultimate—and nothing is, save the living God—then we are caught in illusion and end up distorting that which we serve and destroying ourselves.

Thus, Saint Paul, in his First Letter to Timothy, which we heard read, says that those who seek to be rich fall into a snare, into many and hurtful desires that plunge them into ruin and destruction (1 Tim 6:9). In contrast, if they serve with their freedom the living God, that right relationship enables the true use and enjoyment of all God's creation. So, Paul continues that if people put their hope not on uncertain riches but on God—if they are content with the food and clothing that comes to them as God's gifts—then they can enjoy the things coming to them from God, and they are free to enrich others with good deeds, being liberal and generous. Thereby, Paul concludes, they lay down a good foundation for the future, so that they may take hold of ("possess") the life which is life indeed (1 Tim 6:19).

And this brings us again to the parable. In contrast to some of Jesus' stories, this one does not let us in on the thoughts or motivations of the characters. Jesus lets their bodies do the talking. When we pay attention to the way they dispose of their bodies, we learn all we need to about whom they serve.

We learn five things about Lazarus. The first is that he was among the poorest of the poor, an urban beggar totally dependent on what others chose to give him. The second is that he was ill, so weak that he was carried by others to the gate and left there, so powerless that dogs could come and lick his sores without protest. The third is that he suffered the frustration of the desperate: he desired to eat the scraps from the rich man's table, but none was offered him. The fourth is that Jesus names him Lazarus, which in the Hebrew means "my God helps," a notably accurate designation in this case. The fifth is that God did help him, placing him after his death in Abraham's bosom, an honored place among God's people. Lazarus himself does nothing. The parable invites the inference that he lived by his name, and that the God in whom he hoped gave him what Paul calls "the life that is real."

What do we learn about the other character? He is given no name, as though Jesus was willing to acknowledge the man's own submersion in his wealth and social class. He is simply "a rich man." But he is not simply rich; he is ostentatiously opulent. He is clothed in the most expensive finery available. He feasts, not once or twice a year, but every day, and that sumptuously. He is, in a word, over-the-top rich. Oh, yes, and we learn this: when he dies, he goes to Hades—no fine wine but much thirst.

It is a neat reversal. Like the poor man who saw the crumbs fall but could not get to them, so now the rich man sees Lazarus far off in Abraham's bosom but cannot get across that great divide. And like Lazarus in his former life, the once-rich man cannot change a thing. He can't even change his arrogant character. Look, there he is in Hades, still acting as lord of the manor, asking the big boss Abraham to "send Lazarus" to do his bidding: Lazarus is to slake the rich man's thirst and is to run as a messenger to the rich man's brothers!

Is this, though, simply a neat reversal, with the poor getting theirs in the next life and switching places with the rich who had their consolation in this life? Was Lazarus fortunate then to have been poor, and the rich man problematic only because he was rich?

The dialogue at the end of the parable suggests otherwise. To the rich man's plea that Lazarus be sent to his brothers so they can avoid his fate, Abraham responds with this statement: "They have Moses and the Prophets. Let them hear them." What do Moses and the Prophets have to do with it? Everything.

If the rich man had read and lived by the teaching found in the law of Moses and in the statements of the prophets, he would have perceived Lazarus as a fellow child of Abraham, a brother, for whom he must care. Everywhere in the law and the prophets there is a constant connection drawn between membership in the covenant and doing justice for the poor. As a Jew—he calls out, after all, "Father Abraham!"—the rich man's refusal to acknowledge the poor man at his gate is self-condemnation. Isn't it intriguing that the rich man apparently did know Lazarus by name and is ready to use it when he needs his help?

The final dialogue makes clear that it was not the fact of the rich man's possessing wealth that condemns him but the way he refused to recognize the needs of a brother and disobeyed the clear commands of God concerning the assistance of the poor within Israel. If his brothers wish to avoid the same destiny, then they must read and heed the same Scriptures that the rich man has ignored.

And here's the last thing we learn about the rich man: he still doesn't get it. Moses and the prophets were not good enough for him, and they won't be good enough for his brothers. The obscenely wealthy deserve a greater display: "No, father Abraham, but if someone goes to them from the dead, they will repent." Abraham's chilling response to this last exhibition of self-indulgent obliviousness is chilling: "If they do not hear Moses and the prophets, neither will they be convinced if someone should rise from the dead."

This warning speaks to every Armani suit on Courtland Avenue dashing through glass corridors on the way to power lunches, while a few doors down the street, the urban homeless wait for their sandwiches at the soup kitchen. And it speaks to us.

And let us, at the end, consider Jesus, who speaks this parable. He is the one for whose birth the world had no room, whose first sermon led his townsfolk to seek his death, who touched leper and lame with the human touch of healing, who depended on the hospitality of others as he wandered without a nest or den or place to lay his head, who when he ate with the powerful challenged them but when he ate with his followers served them at table, who broke the bread of his body and poured out the blood of his love.

This is the Jesus who was himself the good news to all the world's poor. This is the Jesus, Luke tells us, of whose suffering Moses and the prophets spoke. This is the Jesus whom, we confess, has been raised from the dead. This is the Jesus who, in his time of testing, embodied the trust expressed by Psalm 91, and who said to the Lord, "My refuge, my fortress, my God, in whom I trust," and for that reason was able to throw away all that he had, all that he was, as gift to the poor and outcast of the world.

And can we, who proclaim this Jesus as raised, any longer walk through any gate, any doorway, without new eyes?

THE MIND OF CHRIST[1]

First Corinthians 8:1–13

My sisters and brothers in Christ, the question "What would Jesus do?"—WWJD—is one of those slogans whose simplicity makes it popular and whose popularity makes it easy to misuse and whose misuse makes it easy to mock. The recent flap over the campaign against SUVs based on the question "What would Jesus drive?" comes to mind.

The slogan, though, has more than simplicity to recommend it. We all know that from the very beginning of the church, not only the power of the Holy Spirit given by the risen Lord but also the memory of the human Jesus have been of fundamental importance in shaping Christian discernment and decision-making. In one form or another Christians have needed, and still need, to ask themselves, "What would Jesus do?"

The limits of the slogan are clear. It is both impossible and irrelevant to literally repeat what Jesus did as a first-century Palestinian Jew. Only Jesus could be the prophet like Moses promised by Deuteronomy. And if Christians are to carry on the battle against demonic forces in their world, they must perform their exorcisms in locales other than the synagogues of Galilee.

Asking what Jesus would do is not the same as asking what Jesus did. It means more than the mechanical imitation of specific words and deeds that remain in the past.

The "would" in "what would Jesus do" introduces a note of condition, and with it, an invitation to imagination. What would Jesus do if Jesus were in this sort of situation? The "would" gives the slogan its real power, for it invites us not to a rigid and predictable reading of a script already written, but to an improvisation based on a character we are trying to play.

---

1. Cannon Chapel, Candler School of Theology, Atlanta, Georgia, January 30, 2003.

The character we are trying to play, of course, is that of Christ. And right here is why Paul is our indispensable help as we try to ask "what would Jesus do." It is Paul who grasped—who knows how?—that the enduring significance of the human Jesus for those given his Spirit is his very character. Not the singular historical facts about Jesus nor the unrepeatable incidents of Jesus' ministry shape us. They stay in the past. What is transferable about Jesus is his character, his *eikon*, or image.

We try to play the character of Jesus because we have been baptized into his body and have been given his Holy Spirit, and the work of that Spirit is to replicate in our freedom the character of Jesus. "Those whom God foreknew," Paul says, "he also predestined to be conformed to the image of His son, so that he might be the first-born of a large family" (Rom 8:29).

The process of playing any character begins with the mind. Method actors ask, "What would this character do in this situation?" They mean, "What would my character think and feel and therefore do in this situation?" They must imagine their way into the character in order to authentically and powerfully represent that character on stage.

The same applies to our playing the character of Christ. Paul tells the Corinthians that they have not received the spirit of the world but the Spirit that comes from God, "so that we might understand the gifts that have been given us by God" (2:12), and he states plainly, "We have the mind of Christ" (2:16).

Acting in a certain way begins with thinking in a certain way. Acting out the character of Christ begins by thinking with Christ's mind.

Much of Paul's two letters to the Corinthians are taken up with his effort to get those first urban Christians from mixed backgrounds and mixed motivations to think the same way about the practical issues of their common life, that is, think together in the way that Jesus thought. But how could they know how Jesus thought? Is the "mind of Christ" simply a neat phrase corresponding to the "body of Christ," or is there a real content to Christ's mind in the way that there are real boundaries to Christ's body?

For Paul, the "mind of Christ" is shorthand for the patterns of self-disposition and action revealed by the cross. The power given to the Corinthians, he says, comes from the weakness of Christ crucified; the wisdom of the Corinthians comes from the foolishness of the cross. The proclamation of the cross is not, for Paul, simply (simply!) how God saved them when human power and human wisdom could not. The pattern of the cross is also to be the hermeneutic of their lives together. They body forth the mind of Christ when they think and act according to the character Jesus revealed in his death.

First Corinthians is so valuable to us because Paul helps us learn how to think this way—not in the abstract, not in the ideal—but in the messiness of real life together, and in the complex instances of sex and food, and with people of differing background and perceptions concerning how the body is and means in matters of eating and mating.

The passage we have read this morning provides an example of how Paul provides a middle term between what Jesus was reported as doing in the Gospels and the difficult moral discernment required of us within a community. He shows the Corinthians—and us—what it means to have the mind of Christ and what it means to embody Jesus' character in circumstances that Jesus himself never faced, within a community made up of diverse persons with fundamentally different points of view.

The differences in perspective among the Corinthians were not trivial. We must remember that first-century Mediterranean people took food as seriously, or perhaps more seriously, than we take sex. Eating together expressed greater intimacy than mating together. And sharing food invited spiritual powers to the table as much as coupling bodies signified spiritual allegiances.

Before they joined the body of Christ, Jews would never eat food that had any association with idolatry, for to eat such food would be to acknowledge the reality of the idols and betray their covenant with the one God. In contrast, before they had joined the body of Christ, gentiles would have eaten food offered to idols and then sold in the market, precisely because such eating offered a share in the power of the gods.

When Jews and gentiles are then joined in the same body of Christ, how shall they eat? Here we have a situation in which the perception of what eating means involves as well a perception of those eating. The Corinthians cannot ask "What did Jesus do?," for despite Jesus' remarkable freedom with regard to table fellowship, Jesus was never in the position of eating with gentiles or sharing meat that had been involved in pagan sacrifice. They need to ask, rather, "What would Jesus do?" if he were in this situation. To put it in Paul's terms, they need to ask how the "mind of Christ" should direct their own dispositions and actions.

Concerning the eating of idol meat as such, Paul expresses no uncertainty. Believers are free to eat whatever is put before them. The reason?

Idols are not real; they have no existence. "There is only one God, from whom all things come and for whom all things exist. And there is only one Lord, Jesus Christ, through whom all things are and through whom they exist" (8:4–6). And if idols are not real, then food offered to them is harmless. Whether you are Jew or Greek, such knowledge gives freedom. Eat with a good and strong conscience.

But now comes the complexity and the need for genuine discernment. According to my own conscience, properly formed by true knowledge, I have every right to eat anything I want. But when I live together with my brothers and sisters in the body of Christ, it is not just a matter of being right but of being righteous, that is, being rightly related both to God and to my neighbor. I live not by myself but with others. Indeed, if I have the mind of Christ, I live not so much for myself as I live for others. The measure of my actions must include the effect my actions have on others. This is new.

My brother or sister's perceptions therefore have a claim on me, even if they are wrong. I may be strong, while they are, for whatever reason, weak. Their own conscience is uncertain or ill-formed, perhaps because their background perceptions continue to hold sway over them. Now, because they see me eat freely, and they know I am strong, they also go ahead and eat, even though they think it wrong to do so. And because under my influence they do what they consider wrong to do, they go against their own conscience and are ruined.

Here is where Paul invokes the mind of Christ revealed in the pattern of the cross. He says, "The weak person is destroyed by your knowledge, the brother or sister for whom Christ died" (8:11). The phrase "brother or sister for whom Christ died" precisely refers to the story of Jesus: Jesus is the one whose character is revealed in a life for others that is perfectly summarized by his death for others. To live by the mind of Christ in this instance, then, to "do what Jesus would do," is to seek not only my own interest but that of my neighbor as well. Or even, to relinquish my own interest lest my neighbor be damaged.

To pursue what I want no matter the effect on my brother or sister is, conversely, to betray the one whose death made our life possible: 'Thus sinning against your brothers and sisters and injuring their weak consciences, you are sinning against Christ." In the former covenant, not eating certain foods constituted loyalty to the one God of Israel. But in the new covenant, acting as though one were not a part of the body of Christ, having dispositions contrary to the mind of Christ, means disloyalty to the God of all peoples.

The mind of Christ demands that in every circumstance we think in terms of others and not simply in terms of ourselves. However good some project might be considered in isolation, the Christian never lives in isolation but always as part of a body. Therefore, Paul says, "If food causes my brother or sister to stumble, I will never eat meat again, so that I do not cause my brother or sister to stumble" (8:13).

Taking 1 Corinthians 8:1–13 as a guide to interpreting the slogan "What would Jesus do?" raises many and difficult questions.

How can we balance the requirement that we act according to our own conscience with the demand that we act to build up the body of Christ? How can we avoid the tyranny of the weak, which threatens all freedom and creativity by refusing to grow in knowledge and strength? How can the strong use their strength to make others strong as well, rather than have their infirmity also weaken us all? How can a community survive if only some of its members act according to the mind of Christ and other members do not? What constitutes a real scandal that causes others to be destroyed as opposed to a shock that challenges them to grow up?

Even asking such questions as a community means that we have moved from the easy use of a slogan to the hard process of thinking within the body. That is a step towards growing up, getting strong, and putting on Christ's mind. As Paul says later in this letter, "Brothers and sisters, do not be children in your thinking. Rather, be infants in evil, but in your thinking, be adults" (14:20).

GOD'S CALL[1]

Isaiah 6:1–10
Psalm 138:1–8
Luke 5:1–11
First Corinthians 15:3–11

My brothers and sisters in Christ, those studying theology instinctively hear the narratives about Isaiah and Peter as stories of God's call to ministry and therefore hear them about themselves. At the moment they are trying to convince boards of ministry that they too have been called to preach, such stories can induce epiphany envy. They say, "If only our call were so crisp, so certain, so directive."

Deep down, we know, of course, that God's call to prophets and apostles is not exactly the same as the call to be a Methodist elder. We know too that scriptural narratives have a way of shaping messy real-life experience into paradigms. Even so, we could use a little more paradigm and a little less mess.

It is true that some people speak as though the call of God were like their daily voice mail. Apparently, their encounter with God/the Holy Spirit/Jesus was the best thing imaginable for their health/business/family life. Before God/Spirit/Jesus, they had sickness, poverty, dysfunctional relationships, lack of meaning. Since their epiphany/call/conversion, they have healing, wealth, loving relationships, and certainty about the path they are to follow. For them, encountering God has been much like finding a good doctor, pension plan, therapist, and life coach.

Why, we may wonder, hasn't it worked that way for us? Why is our call so obscure, our lives such a disaster area, our future so unsure? Why, the more we stay with this odd conviction that someone is summoning us,

1. Cannon Chapel, Candler School of Theology, Atlanta, Georgia, 2005.

do we grow increasingly aware of how inadequate we are to anything God might have in mind?

A closer look at the passages we have heard can prove both reassuring and more than a little frightening. Be careful what you wish for.

Isaiah, we note, already had a career as a prophet when he saw the Lord in the temple, had in fact just finished one of his best poems, the song of the vineyard. And, according to Luke, Simon was already a companion of Jesus before this fishing incident—Jesus had just healed his mother-in-law in his house. The stories we have just heard are less descriptions of how God calls people than depictions of what God's call might entail. That's why Paul's words to the Corinthians about the good news—the one in which they are standing and which is saving them, the one about Jesus' death and resurrection—and about his own call to be an apostle, fall intriguingly across the stories of Isaiah and Simon Peter, inviting us to consider the significance of their intersection.

Isaiah did not change his message after his encounter with the Holy One. Then how did that meeting change him? He learned in that encounter the infinite distance between his own words and the power of God. His lips were burned by the brand from the altar. His words, he learned, would not be understood or accepted. And he would still need to keep speaking them until the land was emptied out, a burnt-over field as bruised as his own blistered lips.

When Jesus tells Peter "don't be afraid, from now on you will be catching people," his wordplay makes a parable of the morning's events. The good news, Peter, is that Jesus will use your skills as a fisher, your abilities as an organizer, your leadership and patience, and put them to use in his project for humans. The less cheerful news is that from your own efforts, you can expect nothing but more long empty nights. When you hear my word, it will seem to contradict much of what you think you know about your business. And when you follow my word, your success will come close to killing you.

Paul alludes only briefly to his own experience of the risen Lord: "Last of all, as though to a miscarried fetus, he appeared also to me . . . but by the grace of God I am what I am, and his grace has not been in vain." As Saul, he had possessed his own sense of calling as the defender of Torah that led him to persecute the church. His calling then seemed to him obvious, his obedience perfect, his direction clear. It was only after his encounter with

Jesus, Acts tell us, that he was struck blind and needed to be led about by the hand.

Paul's self-designation in this statement is shocking. Aristotle speaks of an *ektroma* as an aborted fetus, a mistake of nature, a monster. Does Paul here reveal some sense of deep self-revulsion, as when he elsewhere speaks of his physical infirmity or the thorn in his side (Gal 4:13; 2 Cor 12:7)? Or is he simply speaking gospel? Is the confident, hubristic Paul reduced by his encounter with Christ to a shaking, slippery, sanguinary, half-dead creature through which God breathes life for others?

Does Paul recognize that the same arrogance and fanaticism that drove him before now has been appropriated by Jesus for ends that Paul himself cannot clearly perceive? Is this what he means when he says he bears on his body the *stigmata* of Jesus (Gal 6:17), or when he speaks of his ministry as a carrying about in his body the death of Jesus, so that the life of Jesus might also be made visible (2 Cor 4:11)?

When the living God took hold of Isaiah and Peter and Paul, their problems were not over. They were just starting. The Letter to the Hebrews reminds us that it is a terrifying thing (a *phoberon*) to fall into the hands of the living God (Heb 10:31). This is not simply because the power of God so far surpasses anything within our feeble grasp that when we are merely touched by it we are reduced to weeping and the plea for this awful might to let us be. It is also because whatever game God is playing with us creatures, it is far, far deeper than anything we can comprehend, much less control or predict. We don't know the moves, we are not even sure if there are rules.

Four corollaries follow from these observations.

Perhaps we ought to be more modest in our claims and in our language about our "call." The decision to pursue a career as a Methodist minister is only a rough analogy to the call of Isaiah and Paul.

Perhaps this course on which we have set ourselves is part of God's game, and perhaps not. One thing is certain. Although we can evaluate each other on the basis of learning and personality and the rudiments of competent management, none of us is in a position to judge the use to which the living God is putting us or anyone else.

Perhaps we come closest to such discernment of our messy and non-paradigmatic stories by learning from these passages that when God is at work, more than casual redecoration of the apartment happens; the walls are knocked down and the foundations are shaken. When God is at work, it is through the wounds that God has inflicted. God did so with Isaiah, God did so with Peter, God did so with Paul. And God does so with us.

Perhaps the final and real point is not how we are doing, but what God is doing. And so we say with the psalmist,

> Great is the glory of the Lord, for though the Lord is high, He regards the lowly, but the haughty He knows from afar. Though I walk in the midst of trouble, thou dost preserve my life; thou dost stretch out thy hand against the wrath of my enemies, and thy right hand delivers me. The Lord will fulfill his purpose for me. Thy steadfast love, O Lord, endures forever. Do not forsake the work of Thy hands.

HOPE IN THE FACE OF DEATH[1]

First Thessalonians 4:13–18

My sisters and brothers in Christ, death extinguishes all hope. Death is the undeniable, inexorable "no" spoken against every fantasy, every dream that things will turn out OK. This is the truth of our human existence, confirmed by universal experience. To deny the reality of death is to deny the truth about ourselves.

When our friends die, we are lonely. When our parents die, we are abandoned. When our children die, we are destroyed. Death does not need to be violent to do violence. However death happens, it breaks everything around it into fragments that can never be fully fitted or patched.

The thought of our own death, however, is impossible to sustain, no matter how much we want to practice *memento mori* as a discipline.

When I was young, I found I could think about death calmly. This was because my body told me that I wasn't really dying. Now that I am old and inescapably closer to death, I find that I can't think about death at all. I can't think of my wife's death before me, although I am increasingly forced to consider every contingency preceding and following her death. As for my own, I cannot think at all. I can stare at it, to be sure, or perhaps more accurately, I can glance at it. But that I should actually cease to exist evades thought altogether. What I term thinking, I find, is actually a kind of grief, involving shock, pain, loneliness, despair: that I should lose this world and that this world should have no place for me—what utter desolation, what complete nullification.

Thus, we have this great fact in common with the ancient Thessalonians to whom Paul wrote, a fact based in our common experience. We too have known death and have known the death of hope.

---

1. Cannon Chapel, Candler School of Theology, Atlanta, Georgia, November 6, 2008.

Otherwise, our circumstances seem so very different from those earliest believers who had turned from the worship of dead idols to the living God and who now waited for Jesus to deliver them from the approaching wrath (1 Thess 1:9–10).

You and I live within the bored habituation of a tradition with a billion or more members all around the globe, a tradition that has survived 2,000 years without any real sense of scandal at Jesus' failure to return. You and I dwell amid powerful institutions, elaborate rituals, embedded practices, complex theologies, and a web of interconnected words and deeds serving to convince us that what we do together is somehow real. How could it have survived so long if it were not real?

The Thessalonians, in contrast, were new members of a newly invented cult. They were few in number. They were isolated from other believers, if even they knew about them. They lacked the sort of institutional supports that come with age and development. They were harried and despised by their neighbors. They had been abandoned by their founder only a few short weeks after being gathered. They had been left with no clear directions as to how they might survive if Jesus did not come soon to rescue them.

And now, they have experienced death as the crusher of their hope.

Paul opened his letter to them with generous praise for their dispositions and behavior, their "work of faith and labor of love and endurance in hope of our Lord Jesus Christ" (1:3). Later in the letters, he reaffirms their excellence in two of these dispositions. They were models of faith for others to imitate (1:6–7). And, "on the subject of mutual charity," Paul says they need no instruction from him since they had been "taught by God to love one another" (4:9). Their faith and love, in short, were fine. Paul did not need to write about them. He needed to write because of their lack of hope. They were grieving, he tells them, as those do who have no hope (4:13).

They had, it appears, placed all their trust in Paul's words concerning the living God. Unlike the dead idols who could not give life, the living God could assure them of life. Jesus would rescue them soon.

But now, people in the small community are dying. Perhaps one, perhaps two. That's enough. Even a single death is convincing in its finality. Two deaths are plenty to suggest that the order of things has not changed. Death is still in charge. The promise of a Rescuer from heaven is empty if the ones we love miss out on the rescue. And if they miss out, how can we have hope that we will not miss out as well?

The Thessalonians grieve as those who have no hope. But worse: not only has this new God been shown as no more a conquerer of death than their old gods, they have cut themselves off from the warm embrace of traditional mourning that their former lives allowed. They had scrambled on the good-news lifeboat to save themselves from shipwreck, and now they discover that the lifeboat itself is sinking. Even more than the death of loved ones, they grieve the loss of meaning.

Paul must therefore pick his words to them carefully. No moment more resists pastoral meddling than this one. None of us wants someone talking theology when our hope in life is dying along with the ones we love.

Yet, Paul must speak. These are the people he has asked to take this risk of leaving their accustomed security and familiar gods to put their trust in the living God. He is the one who has left them in their peril.

He longs to be with them, because he knows that his personal presence can speak more powerfully than any words he can write. Unable to visit, he has sent his beloved delegate Timothy to assure them of his care. Still, they need to hear from him—a letter, after all, is a form of personal presence, a way of again experiencing the teacher whose physical distance must not be confused with indifference.

With considerable delicacy, then, Paul addresses the grief the Thessalonians are experiencing over the loved ones who have died. He assures them that the dead will not miss out on the triumph to come. Indeed, the dead in Christ will rise, gather with those still alive, and meet the Lord in the air—so will all be with the Lord forever. Although grief at human death is unavoidable, those who are in Christ are not utterly lost. They have a future with the living and with the Lord.

But on what basis can Paul offer this hope in the midst of death? He subtly reminds them of the first part of the good news he preached to them. They have been focusing on the expectation of Jesus as future rescuer. But Paul's first message had been that Jesus himself had been raised from the dead by the living God (1:10). The heart of Paul's consolation, then, is not the scenario concerning the future—indeed, with his warnings about obsession with timetables, he clearly thinks that this is the wrong place for them to focus (5:1–3).

The heart of Paul's consolation is his reminder of the most basic conviction that drew them into the community, "since we believe that Jesus died and rose again, even so, through Jesus, God will bring with him those who have died" (4:14). The good news of Jesus' resurrection grounds all

Christian hope. The Thessalonians' hope is not based on an expectation of what might happen, but on the recognition of what has already happened. Their loved ones will be raised because Jesus has been raised; Jesus has been raised because God is not a dead projection of human desires but the living God.

The expression of their hope is a life fully aware, fully alert. They are not in darkness but in the day; they are not asleep but awake; they are not drunk but sober. They can therefore put on, in addition to the breastplate of faith and love, "the helmet that is the hope for salvation" (5:8). God has not destined them for wrath, Paul assures them, "but for obtaining salvation through our Lord Jesus Christ, who died for us, so that whether we are awake or asleep we may live with him" (5:10). They will be with the Lord always (4:17), Paul assures them, because the Lord is already with them always.

Paul's pastoral concern for his young and fragile community can be learned from his exhortation in 4:18, "therefore encourage/comfort/exhort one another with these words," that he repeats in 5:11: "Therefore encourage one another and build one another up, as indeed you are doing."

No one of them alone can hold onto a hope that flies in the face of the evidence given by their own bodies and by the universal experience of the world. They must build their distinct and contrarian vision of hope through the slow and patient practice of mutual reinforcement, mutual witness, not when all is going well and the enemy seems far distant but, most of all, when the enemy is within the gates and appears to be winning.

We who gather here this morning are no less fragile in our hope than were the ancient Thessalonians. It is just harder for us to get in contact with that fragility because it is so well covered over by layers of unexamined and inattentive habit. We are just as likely as they were to grieve as do those without hope, isolated by the pain brought by death and the devastation of our fond expectations. Each of us alone easily succumbs to the overwhelming fact of our loss, feeling that we too are lost.

We too are liable to forget that the presence of the resurrected one among us is the truth that counters, and identifies as a lie, the contradictory truth of our experience that death extinguishes all hope. That is why we gather as we do today, precisely to read these words from Scripture and remind each other of the truth that none of us can grasp individually and requires all of us to hold it at all, namely, that death is not the destroyer of all hope, that death has already been used by God as the instrument of hope through the resurrection of our Lord Jesus Christ.

THE BEGINNING OF WISDOM[1]

Proverbs 1:1–7
Psalm 139:1–18
Luke 12:4–12

M y sisters and brothers in Christ, Scripture states confidently and without equivocation that fear of the Lord is the beginning of wisdom (Prov 1:7). It is a statement worth pondering for those of us who profess to have something to do with wisdom, and, for that matter, with the Lord.

What kind of fear is this? In what sense is it a beginning? And how can fear be essential to the path to wisdom?

Our reflection is both more necessary and more difficult because our generation instinctively recoils at any mention of fear, even while our mass media and social networks evoke fear on every side. Headlines scream of explosions by terror-mongering ideologues that paralyze cities with suspicion and fear. Attending public events occasions deep anxiety: Will we be the targets of random slaughter or purposeful execution?

Terror numbs us even as it enthralls us. We suspect and dread the other as enemy even as we are unable to identify exactly who among the other is the enemy. Governments suspect other states of spying and plotting terror because they themselves spy and plot terror. Governments also suspect their own citizens of sedition, while citizens live in fear that their elected officials spy on them and seek to suppress their freedom.

Such public and political fear by no means exhausts the catalogue of anxieties that beset us and from which we long to be free. Fear is chronic and quotidian. We fear both the shadow and the too-bright light. We fear the heights from which we might fall and the depths from which we may never crawl. We fear both loss and gain; we fear failure and also success.

---

1. Spring Semester Convocation, my last sermon to the faculty, staff, and students at Candler. Cannon Chapel, Candler School of Theology, Atlanta, Georgia, January 2016.

Above all, we fear being judged by others.

Students fear professors because the professors might discover how ignorant the students are. Professors fear students because students might find out how dull and narrow the professors are. Professors fear administration—they might not get tenure. Administration fears accreditors—maybe they should not have granted tenure. Physicians fear their patients—they might get sued. Patients fear the medical system—they might get screwed.

Fear is the mighty motor that builds walls and ramparts between us; fear drives the mechanisms of camouflage and deception that leave us isolated in perpetual alertness; we may be found out, we may be known, we might be discovered; and once discovered, judged; and once judged, dismissed, hurt, or abandoned.

How we long for the perfect love, which, as John tells us, drives out fear (1 John 4:18)! How we wish that Jesus' words to his followers, "Do not be afraid" (Luke 5:10), might also govern our lives and our world! How we crave having such a friend in Jesus, that fear—fear of each other, fear of ourselves, fear of discovery, fear of judgment, fear of punishment—might have no more power over us!

But look! It is Jesus himself who declares in this Gospel reading, "I tell you, my friends, do not fear those who kill the body and after that can do nothing more," meaning, do not fear other humans; "but I will tell you whom to fear: fear Him who, after He has killed, has power to cast into hell" (Luke 12:4), meaning, fear God. It is Jesus himself who tells us that it is God whom we need fear. Some friend!

Jesus' statement, though, accords with the constant witness of Scripture. The One we should fear is the One who at every moment creates us out of nothingness and, as our Creator, calls us to account.

The fear of God, then, connects to the conviction that God is judge—indeed, our judge—and this conviction depends on the truth that God creates everything that exists at every moment and that the living God knows our hearts at every moment. God has maker's knowledge of all that is. God knows what is in the process of being created, from the inside. If God is not Creator of the world in this strong sense, then there can be no real meaning to the proposition that God is judge, nor any real reason to fear the Lord.

To confess that God is judge, however, does not mean that we know *how* God judges. We are as thoroughly in the dark as anyone else concerning God's ways in the world. We observe with the same anguish as everyone else the suffering of the righteous and the arrogance of the oppressor. No more than anyone else can Christians supply the positive contents of their confession. We have no more information than the unbeliever on heaven *or* hell, on the establishment of a righteous kingdom. We have no better evidence than they for the hope that possesses us.

But our confession that God is our judge has little to do with the *how* of God's judgment and everything to do with the *that* of his judgment. We have no definition for the manner God in which restores right relations, but we assert that God rightly knows what those relations are. The heart of this confession is that God is the discerner of hearts (Acts 1:24).

Thus, by calling God our judge, we mean that God judges us here and now. All that we think and say and do lies before the all-seeing eye of God (Heb 4:12–13). The practice of the presence of God is simply opening ourselves to the gaze of the One who already sees us as we truly are. Although we may be opaque to ourselves and a puzzle to others, we are transparent to the One who makes us. God knows us utterly, knows us rightly at every moment, at this moment.

In every encounter between humans, then, and in every encounter of humans with the world, the truth of that encounter is known only by its silent and unseen enabler. And more: even when I am most alone, I lie open to the gaze of God, my heart is discerned by God; I am known far more completely and truly by God than I know myself.

Such a realization is a source of genuine and deep fear. It is also the basis for true wisdom.

It is the source of authentic fear. Our deepest human longing, it would seem, is to be truly known by another, but such longing evokes a scary prospect: If we are known truly by another human, will we not be rejected as unworthy? Here is the workshop for all our projects of camouflage and deception: we seek the acceptance of others by manufacturing a self of our own construction that hides as much as possible of the terrified child behind the mask. But such hiding is not possible from the One who makes us and knows us from the inside. The psalmist declares, "If I say, 'Surely the darkness shall cover me, and the light around me become night,' even the darkness is not dark to you, the night is as bright as the day, the darkness is as light to you" (Ps 139:11–12).

It is also the basis of true wisdom, for it recognizes the infinite qualitative distance between Creator and creature: God is God, and we are not. Jean-Paul Sartre complained that the "stare" of other people reduces us to an object. The confession of God as judge asserts the exact opposite. To be known (seen) by the One who is truly Other and draws us at this moment into existence establishes us as subjects.

It is, in fact, God's gaze that gives us the freedom to be ourselves as God makes us rather than the prisoner of other people's perceptions of us. It is also because we are transparent to the gaze of God that we can afford to be honest with ourselves. We can let ourselves admit what is already known to the only One who counts. Acceptance of God's discernment of our hearts is to accept God's acceptance of us as his creatures.

Such fear of the Lord liberates us, in turn, with regard to the opinions of others—whether positive or negative, whether laudatory or condemnatory—as profoundly irrelevant. Of what ultimate significance are judgments that are based only on appearances and distorted by the bias of the observers?

Standing under the judgment of God, all measurements of success and failure fall away, except this one: Am I speaking and writing and acting in service to the truth as it has been given to me to bear witness?

The denial of God's judgment here and now leads, in turn, to the corruption of wisdom. If God is not judge, after all, humans must assume the entire responsibility for justice being done in the world. If God can't do it, we must. Someone must reward the good and punish the wicked. And since we have no heaven or hell in our control, we must accomplish justice right here and right now. Vengeance and retribution are thereby legitimated, indeed, demanded.

Tragically, we are unable to do it. Humans cannot do justice in all the world, for they do not see all things and see them truly. They do not understand the workings of their own hearts, much less the hearts of others. They can only observe the surface of things and must therefore judge by appearances alone, which is precisely how Scripture defines corrupt judgment (see Lev 19:15). Humans find themselves in the impossible situation of bearing an infinite divine responsibility while having only a limited human capability.

The declaration "'vengeance is mine, I will repay,' says the Lord" (Deut 32:35; Rom 12:19) does not tell us how God's justice will be accomplished, but it does relieve us of a terrible responsibility we were never capable of fulfilling. In his Letter to the Romans, Paul states the situation succinctly: "Who are you to pass judgment on another's servants? It is before their Lord that they will stand or fall" (14:4), and he continues, "Why do you pass judgment on your brother or sister? Or you, why do you despise your brother or sister? For we will all stand before the judgment seat of God, for it is written, 'As I live, says the Lord, every knee shall bow to me, and every tongue shall give praise to God.' So, then, each one of us will be accountable to God" (14:10–12).

Even more intimate truths are distorted when we deny God's judgment. Why should we care about the sincerity of our intentions, if they are not known by the One who discerns correctly and without bias? Purity of heart is an ideal only if our intentions and not simply our actions count. With one stroke, denying God as our judge destroys the reason for interior integrity. Why be sincere, if all that can be observed by others is appearance? If all that counts is joining the right movement or marching for the right cause—and what else could count if my only judges are my fellow dim-sighted humans—then why should I not be hypocritical?

Why not be racist in my most secret thoughts while parading in public my affirmations of diversity? Why not be sexist in my inner self, so long as I keep this disposition camouflaged by politically correct gestures?

For that matter, why should we go into an inner room to pray to the God, who, Jesus tells us, hears what is said in secret (Matt 6:6), so long as we celebrate noisily with others in common rituals? What possible meaning could there be to the prayer of silence if there is not the Other before whom my heart is laid bare?

Having such a fear of God in our hearts is required of each one of us as we begin another semester of academic work that professes to be about the pursuit of wisdom.

Those of us in this place who teach and write for publication should do so in the awareness that our every word, act, and inflection of our heart lie open to the gaze of the One who creates us. We may be able to fool students, and readers, and even reviewers, but if we fail to strive for integrity in all our speech and writing, we already stand condemned by the word of truth.

Those of us who are students in this place should likewise read and research and write in the awareness that the integrity required of us is not measured by our reputation among our fellow students or by the mark given by the teacher, but by the judgment of God. Does our work seek the truth? Have we witnessed faithfully to what our mind sees? We can fool the teacher and fool our fellow students, but we cannot fool God.

Those of us who enable the work of this school through administration or staff support should likewise know that it is not the approval of supervisor or donor or client that counts but the approval of the unseen judge who discerns our hearts.

For all of us in this school of theology pledged to the service of God's people, seeking to live by any standard less than the fear of the Lord is truly to turn from the path of wisdom.

SERMONS TO SCATTERED
ASSEMBLIES

GOD IS AN OPEN QUESTION[1]

Exodus 17:8–13
Second Timothy 3:14–17
Luke 18:1–8

My brothers and sisters in Christ, we come here week after week when our friends are asleep or reading the Sunday paper. We don't come expecting to be distracted or entertained. We come because we expect to hear a word different from our own.

We are all too familiar with our own words. They fill our heads and spill out of our mouths and make walls of noise around our fear of silence. That's our word. We know it. We expect no life from it.

No, we come together to hear God's word.

We do this because we are well aware of how broken and piecemeal our own lives and language are.

Most of the time we really don't know what we are doing. We're happy to find we are still putting one foot in front of another.

We may suspect that there is some meaning to all the odd and random moments of our days and weeks and all-too-short years. We have heard there is some meaning to it all, but we can't get at it with our own words. Our speech is too muddled and confused. Our lives are too split and broken.

So, we come here, even on a gray and drizzly morning like this one, when it would seem better to stay in bed or toast our feet at a fire. We come to hear a word which will shape our own speech, to find a pattern to the everyday madness of our lives, to allow ourselves for a moment to be silent and listen, expecting—what?

We expect first of all what we hear in this reading from Paul's Second Letter to Timothy, that because this word is inspired by God it will be for us, as it was for Timothy, profitable; it will train us in righteousness, complete

1. First Presbyterian Church, Bedford, Indiana, 1983.

us, equip us for every good work. We expect from this word our "instruction in salvation through faith in Jesus Christ."

In short, we expect from the word we hear more than our own words can supply; we expect a meaning to our madness, a strength to support our weakness, an answer to our questions.

With such high expectations, we cannot but be disappointed at times like today when the word of Scripture seems as confused as our own. We listen attentively. We do not hear a smooth and satisfying answer to our questions but a larger question in return, perhaps a hard question, perhaps one we do not want to hear.

We start off well enough in the first reading from Exodus. It presents a stirring assurance. Moses holds aloft the staff and—we understand—commands God's presence among the troops of the Israelites against the Midianites. So long as Moses' arms hold up, the Lord fights for Israel. This, we think, is how religion should work. This, we imagine, is how prayer should operate. How straightforward. How rewarding. How much like what we want God to be. How much, in fact, like our own word does this word seem.

And therefore, perhaps, a bit suspicious. Have we met a Moses lately? Do we have such a staff? Do our arms reach into heaven and command the Lord's assistance, so that all the many enemies we fight every day (our sloth, deadly boredom, envy, pain, fear, and confusion)—do these flee from us because the mighty warrior, the Lord, is on our side? Perhaps for you. Not for me.

So, I hear this word from long ago, this tale of Moses and the staff, as a lesson for my instruction. It tells me: God is real and powerful to help. God does respond to prayer.

But I cannot hear it completely, for I am no Moses, have no staff and sometimes not even a prayer. And so I doubt: is God real in the way the story says? Is this really how faith works? If I don't have a magic stick, if my arms don't shake the clouds and make them rain prosperity and peace for those I love, is this because I lack faith or because God lacks faithfulness? Is God's word here a deceiving word? Or am I a self-deceiving hearer?

With some sense of relief, then, we turn to Jesus' parable in Luke 18:1–8. Doesn't Jesus speak clearly in these stories of his about the nature of God's kingdom? Are not his words healing? Do they not cut through the fictions and fantasies of the old dispensation and state with calm authority the will of his Father?

Such is our expectation, and indeed, the evangelist introduces the parable with this helpful note: "He told them a parable to the effect that they ought always to pray and not lose heart." Surely, then, we will now hear a validation for prayer that comes closer to our own experience than Moses on the mountain and the slaughtered hordes below.

What does Jesus teach us about the rewards of constant prayer? He tells us a rather odd story about a widow and a judge. We recognize the situation: poor old woman, uncaring bureaucrat. Familiar territory to anyone who has met a magistrate or dealt with the DMV. How does the story run? The bureaucrat attends to the woman's lawsuit even though he is not in the least interested, because she wears him down.

Wait a minute! Let's parse the story: if we are to understand the poor widow as us, then the unjust judge must be God. Is this what we want to learn about God? Is this the same God Jesus told us about, before whom no flowers die, and no sparrows fall to earth, and no hairs grow, without his care? Is God, then, a mean old magistrate who has to be irritated into a response?

Maybe. But the point is not whether he cares. Jesus tells us, "Listen to what the unrighteous judge says." He *will* vindicate. The story does not tell us *how*. The story does not tell us whether it was done *gently*. The story does not tell us the widow was vindicated *in exactly the way she wanted*. Only that it was done. God does respond to prayer.

But here precisely is the problem. It is *God* who responds to prayer. Irritating God into a response means that we have opened ourselves to the One about whom the Letter to the Hebrews remarks, "It is a fearful thing to fall into the hands of the living God" (Heb 10:31).

We do not possess a marvelous wand with which to control events. Prayer is not magic. God is not a vending machine. When we ask him to enter our lives, God might—no, probably will—come in and kick down the walls, scattering the neatly arranged furniture of our own ideas and plans, even our idea of who God is, even our plan of how to love him. God is like the man from the appliance store who busts down our door with an oversized refrigerator and says, "You the one who wanted this vindication delivered?"

That is why Jesus concludes with a question: "Will the Son of Man find faith on earth?" It is an open question, one that each of us must answer in our lives. Jesus knew, I think, that we would much rather have a God whom we could control by our prayers, like Moses with his magic staff. We would ask, God would give—in the manner and measure of our request: we want that burger with the works, but skip the mayo. But Jesus tells us, God is not like that. If you truly want a living God, you must get used to dealing with a God who answers in his own way, who seeks only to vindicate you, not to please and delight you at the same time.

Maybe this is why we don't pray with faith. Maybe we don't keep kicking at God's door because we have learned Jesus' lesson. God might awake, rise with his mighty arm, and vindicate his elect, and speedily. But we may not really want it on his terms.

So, we leave these words this morning not with an answer but a question, a hard question put to our lives. But then, we have grown used to that.

THE KINGDOM OF GOD AND POLITICAL CHOICES[1]

Isaiah 25:1–10
Matthew 22:1–14

M y sisters and brothers in Christ, the presidential campaign swirling around us has challenged those calling themselves Christians to reconsider some difficult questions. This campaign has focused to perhaps an unprecedented degree on the personal religious beliefs of the candidates and how they might translate their convictions into public policy across a spectrum of social issues, the most notorious being abortion, disarmament, school prayer, and social welfare programs.

During debates over these issues, various statements have been made concerning the relationship between religion and public morality. And it is certainly appropriate for us to ask: What *is* the connection between one's Christian commitment and one's attitude toward social structures and programs? Or, to use much more traditional language, what is the relationship between the kingdom of God and the social order? This is a perennial problem, which must be resolved again and again, always provisionally, by every generation.

Thinking it through is not made any easier by the simplistic and one-sided answers given by the politicians themselves.

From one side, we are informed that the kingdom of God is all about care and compassion for the weak ones in our society. Certainly—inarguably—that is an element in God's rule. But when such dispositions toward the weak are identified with specific governmental programs, one rightly hesitates.

1. First Presbyterian Church, Bedford, Indiana, 1984.

From the other side, similarly, we hear the confident assertion that the kingdom of God consists in keeping traditional moral codes and in recognizing God's claim over individual lives. This too is surely right. But do such convictions translate immediately into legislative programs banning abortion or mandating prayer in public schools?

The political climate, in short, is far more conducive to spouting slogans than to careful thinking. It is an atmosphere which encourages the reduction of God's rule to an ideology. In such an atmosphere, it is harder, but also the more necessary, for Christians to give hard and deliberate thought to this critical issue of the relationship between the kingdom of God and the social order.

Following our natural Christian inclination, we turn to the Scriptures for guidance, but we find little that is helpful in any obvious way. The main reason is simple enough. The New Testament writings simply do not address such issues directly. They were composed, after all, for a small and persecuted minority that could never have imagined itself as a significant player in the larger world. The messianic movement was a tiny and powerless segment within the enormous, overwhelming rule of the Roman Empire. Rome might be now hostile, now benign, but it was always so imposingly present that it was universally regarded as a fact of nature, like the sunrise or the mountains. The Christian writings were turned instead to the difficult-enough task of building the community of believers. Given life by the resurrection of Jesus, it now awaited the definitive revelation of God's rule at his return.

When we do catch a glimpse of the larger political world, it is always from the perspective of those who are being either well or ill treated by this unquestioned and unquestionable world order. Thus, in the context of protection by the state, we find it spoken of with approval by Luke-Acts, by Paul's Letter to the Romans, and by the First Letter of Peter. Such approval had nothing to do with the morals of the emperor or the organization of welfare for the poor. Only when the state became a force inimical to the free practice of the Christian life was it seen as a beast and a destroyer, as in the book of Revelation. This writing regarded the empire negatively because it arrogated to itself an allegiance that humans could give only to God and so revealed itself as an enemy of God's rule.

Thus, the New Testament writings are diverse and fragmentary. They are not capable of directly addressing the complex issues we face as citizens of this country during the present election season.

Does this mean that Scripture is utterly silent? Not at all. Even if it cannot speak directly to our issues by way of command, it can speak to us obliquely by way of metaphor and parable.

Such is the case with the words of Jesus today in Matthew's Gospel, in the parable of the king who gave a wedding feast for his son. Jesus makes clear that he intends the parable to be heard as a teaching about the kingdom of God. He did not innovate in making the comparison but tapped into a long tradition. We heard in today's first reading from the prophet Isaiah, for example, that God's rule over the world will involve "a feast of fat things, a feast of wine on the lees, of fat things full of marrow" (Isa 25:6). Such comparisons nurtured definite expectations about God's future rule. It would be one in which those who belonged to him would be vindicated, and those opposed to him punished. It would be overwhelmingly obvious in its appearance. It would give a special place of honor to the elect.

In light of such expectations, Jesus' parable is surprising, even disturbing. He does not speak of the enjoyment of good things. The parable is much darker. The king's invitation can be refused, even violently, making us wonder about the actual power of the king. But then we learn that those who refused are themselves violently destroyed. This makes us feel better about the king's power, but it also makes us wonder about his sanguinary disposition. Can even the death of a son justify the destruction of a city and its inhabitants?

Still more shocking is the final scene, which is unique to Matthew's version of this parable. One of the guests who accepted the invitation and came to the banquet is thrown "into the outer darkness." Even if we accept the view that guests would ordinarily be given a wedding garment at the door, so that the man's carelessness appears as a deliberate affront to the king's hospitality, we still are stunned by the sudden and brutal turn of events. It is not a comforting story. What are we to make of it?

Jesus' parables do not yield neat political or religious slogans. Instead, they shake us into thinking; they force us to consider once more just who it is with whom we think we are involved when we speak blithely of "God's kingdom." In this parable of threat and rejection, we learn again that it is a terrible thing to fall into the hands of the living God (Heb 10:31). This parable is, in fact, no less terrible.

We can guess at the effect Jesus wanted to create when he first spoke the parable during his ministry. He was surrounded by hostile listeners. Surely he saw himself as the son who was being rejected. And he made it plain to those who refused his call that they too would on that account be rejected.

It is also possible to see how Matthew understood this parable that he received from the church's tradition. He too undoubtedly saw it as an interpretation of the entire ministry of Jesus: the one God sent as a Son to invite people into his kingdom was rejected by his own people and killed. In Matthew's view, they deserved the punishment they received (see Matt 27:25).

But is the parable only a story about the past? Can it challenge us still today? Yes, for it is the word of the living God, and just as he calls us daily, moment by moment, out of our complacency into question, so does his word in Scripture sharpen and clarify that call. But how does it speak? In tones that should shatter our smugness and shake our presumption.

It tells us, first, that the kingdom of which we speak is not a human construction. It is not fitted to our predilections or prejudices. It is not molded to our morality or mores. It is the word of the living God, and we understand neither him nor his ways (Rom 11:33–36). No one is in the right with God. Every creature is laid bare to his gaze (Heb 4:12–13). Every human is called by him to a response and a decision. God's kingdom is not a comfortable home for us to decorate and sit in comfortably. It is a challenge that moves always before us and demands that we move into the dangerous spaces of God's own freedom.

The parable reminds us, second, that our decision with regard to God's call has deadly consequences. No other decision can be compared to this one. This is the only truly ultimate decision, the commitment to serve under the rule of God. On it hinges our life. If we have decided rightly, we gain a share in God's own life. If we have decided wrongly, even this mortal life has been one of foolishness and waste.

The parable reminds us, third, that even those who have once responded, who have once committed themselves to God's rule, must still respond again and again, for the response is to the living God whose call is new every day (see Heb 3:7–19). Even for those in the messianic community, refusal and rejection are still possible. The wedding garment signifies this: that there is no end to deciding for God's rule in this world.

All well and good. But do such conclusions help guide us as we make social and political decisions? Do they help us determine appropriate plans and policies? No. Scripture does not give us this assistance. Why? Because such norms cannot be spelled out for every time and circumstance, for the kingdom is not one of planning and program, but one of response to the new and surprising revelation of God in every time and place and circumstance.

Do we have nothing, then, to guide us through the current debates? Are we left with only the reminder that our decisions are consequential, with no light thrown on deciding? Not entirely.

Jesus speaks elsewhere about the kingdom, and two of his statements bear significantly on the issues of the present campaign.

One of these sayings is also by way of parable. Jesus pictures the last judgment carried out by the Son of Man (Matt 25:31–48). He separates the sheep and the goats, sending some to reward and some to punishment. All are surprised when he tells them the measure for judgment. They had either fed him when he was hungry and clothed him when he was naked and visited him when he was in prison, or they had not. When each group protests that they had not seen him in those circumstances, he says, "Insofar as you did it for one of these little ones, you did it to me." Here is a serious measure for behavior in God's kingdom. We cannot claim to be living under God's rule while ignoring the need to care for society's outcast, poor, neglected, and weak.

But Jesus has other words as well concerning "these little ones," now with reference to the acceptance of children: "Whoever receives one such child in my name accepts me"; and again, with reference to the corruption of children, "Whoever causes one of these little ones who believes in me to sin, it would be better for him to have a great millstone fastened around his neck and to be drowned in the depth of the sea" (Matt 18:5–6); and again, "It is not the will of my Father who is in heaven that one of these little ones shall perish" (Matt 18:14). Here is another norm for behavior in God's kingdom. We cannot claim to be living under God's rule when we systematically cut off the life of children or corrupt them.

Heresy consists in the selection of one truth to the distortion of others. Ideology is a partial truth used to justify some programs to the exclusion of other programs.

In the present season it is important, though admittedly difficult, for thoughtful Christians to recognize that Jesus' proclamation of God's kingdom transcends all simplistic reductions of it, and that we who participate in the hard decisions concerning our common life do so under the judgment of God.

THE QUALITY OF WAITING[1]

James 5:7–9

My brothers and sisters in Christ, I would like to think with you a bit this morning about this short passage from the Letter of James that we have heard. This is not one of those prophetic-sounding passages—like the one just before the one we read (5:1–6) in which James attacks the rich landowners who oppress their laborers. Here James speaks to those of us he calls "brothers and sisters," and his words are quiet, if no less stern.

James reminds us of a basic truth about our existence as Christians, when he declares in three different ways: "the Lord is coming," and "the Lord is near," and "the judge is standing at the gate." He reminds us that we live in an in-between time. God changed all of history when he raised Jesus as Lord from the dead. But we still await his glorious revelation as judge.

The conviction that Jesus will return as judge is as ancient and fundamental a belief as that in the resurrection itself. Yet we can hardly find any two Christians who agree on exactly what that conviction actually means.

Some believers get so wrapped up in this future expectation that they make it the whole of their religion. They obsess over the times and seasons of Jesus' return. It's almost as though that final victory was all that was important, as though God had not already fundamentally triumphed over sin and death through the resurrection of Jesus and the gift of the Holy Spirit.

Other believers go the other way. For them, an expectation of Jesus' return is like a religious appendix. It is a vestigial organ that can be removed at no great cost. They treat belief in a future triumph of God as a quaint fantasy. They prefer to think about the victory of God in terms of social progress and reform.

The problem with both extremes is that they focus on the *how* of Jesus' coming. James reminds us that the important thing is the *that* of his return.

---

1. Mount Gilead Church of Christ, Brown County, Indiana, August 4, 1985.

In whatever fashion, there is more of Jesus we have yet to experience. We live between the "already" and the "not yet."

Why is this reminder important? Because we need to be told over and over who we are and to whom we belong. Left to ourselves, we are all too eager to act as though we belonged to ourselves and were masters of our own lives. And as long as things go well—as long as we are healthy and prosperous, this illusion can work. But it is an illusion.

Our conviction that the Lord will return as judge reminds us of this simple truth: we came from God; he created us; we are answerable to him. He is the judge.

The point of the *parousia*, of Jesus' return, is not what is going to happen in that future event but how we are to live now. This is why James tells us the judge is at the gates. He does not mean this in a temporal sense. Jesus was "at the gates" 2,000 years ago, and he is "at the gates" now. He is near and is our judge, and our lives should be lived as though under his judgment.

We are not, after all, like people who are waiting for a train to arrive, or for the washing machine to finish its spin cycle. That sort of waiting is empty time. Our waiting for the Lord is not empty time but full time. We already share in the victory of God through the gift of the Holy Spirit. This in-between time ought, then, to be lived as though waiting for One who is, in the most important way, already with us—more like waiting for a best friend to return from an errand.

How does James want us to spend this in-between time? He tells us three times, "be patient." Patience is an obvious virtue for those who wait. James's instruction reminds us of Jesus telling his disciples "by your patience you will gain your lives" (Luke 21:19). The fascinating thing about James's command is that he uses a very unusual term for "patience." Rather than the Greek word meaning "to endure," he uses a term meaning "to be long-suffering . . . or tolerant." The term he uses is ordinarily used for people like judges, and in Scripture it is used primarily for God as judge: God is long-suffering with humans. So, in the Second Letter of Peter, we are told that God's long-suffering is for the purpose of our repentance (2 Pet 3:9). The long-suffering or tolerance of God means that God gives humans time and space for the exercise of their freedom. God gives them room to make choices for or against him.

But what does it mean for James to tell *us* to be long-suffering until the coming of the Lord? Three things. First, he means that we are to do more than simply endure with gritted teeth, as if we were in empty time. Second, he means that we should act toward each other as God acts toward us. Third, we are to give each other time and space for freedom until the coming of the Lord.

As we would expect from this down-to-earth teacher, James has some practical advice on the quality of our patience or long-suffering.

He tells us first that we are not to hold grudges against each other. This is a better translation of the Greek than "do not grumble against each other." When we hold grudges, James says, we bring judgment on ourselves. There is psychological truth here, isn't there? People who are having a rough time often want to take it out on others. When we are hurt, we want to hurt others in return. And we love to hold grudges. We arrest, try, and convict others and banish them to a prison far from our affection or goodwill. When we do this, though, we act like an unjust judge without long-suffering. James wants us to act toward each other as God acts toward us. In another place he tells us, "You should so speak and act as those who will be judged by the law of freedom; for judgment is without mercy to the one who shows no mercy; mercy, on the other hand, overcomes even judgment" (1:12).

Second, James shows us how we can be long-suffering toward each other. He says, "Establish your hearts, for the Lord is near." It is because God is near to us and shows us such mercy that we are able to show mercy toward each other. This is why we should "fix our hearts" not on the faults of others, which drive us to distraction, but on the mercy of the Lord that sustains us even when we test it most sorely. When James says the Lord is near, we remember he does not mean merely in terms of time. The Lord is present now in the power of the Spirit. He is nearer to us than our own hearts and can sustain us. In the presence of the one who will one day mysteriously show himself as our judge, we show mercy to each other, confident that the Lord will indeed measure us by the measure by which we ourselves have measured.

Third, James tells us to wait for the Lord's coming with the kind of patience a farmer displays when waiting for a crop. The farmer, he says, waits through both the early and the late rain, knowing that something alive and powerful is there in the earth. Thus our waiting for the Lord can be calm and full of confidence, because the seed of God's own word has been sown in our hearts—James speaks of it as the "implanted word that can save your souls" (1:21), and as Jesus tells us in Luke's Gospel, "The ones in good soil are those who hearing the word hold it fast in an honest and good heart and bring forth fruit in patience" (Luke 8:15).

My sisters and brothers, in this season of late summer, when heat and humidity sometimes drive us to distraction, when small faults and failure become magnified, when it is easy to hold a grudge against each other, it is helpful to remember these words of James that we have heard this morning. In another part of his letter, James tells us, "Let every person be quick to hear, slow to speak, slow to anger, for human anger does not work the righteousness of God" (1:19–20). And he returns once more to a summertime image when he declares, "The harvest of righteousness is sown in peace by those who make peace" (3:16). Let us, then, since the Lord is near and at the very gates, fix our hearts on him and, at the same time, expand them in mercy and peace toward each other.

THE COST OF COMPASSION[1]

Second Timothy 2:8–13
Mark 1:40–45

My brothers and sisters in Christ, faith is not a matter of what we believe but a matter of how we act. Christianity does not mean having faith in Jesus so much as it means imitating the faith of Jesus. When we study a Gospel story, then, we seek the pattern to our own lives, as it was enacted first in the life of Jesus. As the Holy Spirit shaped him as servant, so does the gift of his Spirit shape us.

Today, the story of Jesus' healing of a leper shows us how faith involves compassion. It shows us as well that compassion has a cost.

The story was undoubtedly told over and over again orally by the first believers long before Mark included it in his Gospel narrative. It was told and retold because, like all the stories about Jesus, it contained in itself the essence of the good news. For all who are in whatever way touched by "leprosy"—all of us who are distanced from others by color, character, or catastrophe, all who bear the stigma of being different and therefore in some way dangerous—the story says that God's compassion is more than strong enough to overcome such human barriers as sickness and social stigma. In the touch of Jesus, we feel the finger of God, reaching across all the chasms of ignorance and prejudice and telling us, "You belong, you are not a stranger." This is already unexpected and very good news.

In Mark's Gospel, however, we do not read this story in isolation. We read it as part of a larger narrative. By doing this, we learn that God's fidelity to us is not a matter of momentary acceptance but is spelled out in the whole pattern of life that was the Messiah's, our Lord Jesus'. When we hear the story as a moment of that life, we can better grasp the nature and the

---

1. First Presbyterian Church, Bedford, Indiana, March 1, 1987.

cost of compassion, both for Jesus and for those of us wishing to follow Jesus.

We note first that the term "compassion" denotes feeling, emotion. Jesus is someone who *feels*. He is not a bloodless icon on the wall. He is a living, lurching human being, who like us feels in his stomach and in his pores, must therefore (like us) manage the rush of adrenaline and the surge of desire.

The term "compassion" also denotes a feeling for and toward another. The word literally means "to suffer with" another. What Jesus felt, then, was not generated from within himself but was in response to another, a feeling with. Such feeling with involves both perception and understanding, what we now call empathy. What did Jesus feel in this case?

He was able to sense the pain and fear that had driven the leprous man to fall at Jesus' knees. He could feel in his own stomach the ache of loneliness and isolation this man must have been experiencing, separated from others because of his affliction, forced to wander in desert places and cry out warning to all passersby lest they be defiled by his very presence. Jesus felt this; what the man felt became *his* feeling.

Then, Jesus touched the man physically. He translated his feeling with, his compassion, into action. Jesus reached his hand across the religious taboo, across the danger of contagion, across the moat of certainly his own fear, and touched him. By that very touch, the man was healed, for the nature of his distress was not, first of all, the discoloration of his skin, but his enforced alienation from human society that his appearance caused. Jesus' touch healed not by magic but by compassion. Nothing so heals as to be understood and accepted in our affliction.

Finally, Jesus says, "I do will it, be made clean." He speaks the words that make explicit his feeling and his action. He has heard the man's plea, "if you will I can be made clean," and has felt what the man felt, and has touched the man's hand, and while so doing he speaks the man's desire and makes it his own. The exchange is complete, and through it, strength flows to weakness, health to sickness, and isolation to community. The man is healed.

By making us think about what Jesus felt and did for the man, Mark forces us to shift our perspective from our own leprosy and need for healing to those around us. He shows us Jesus as the one whom we are to follow. As he did, so are we called to do. Then, we must ask, who are the lepers who approach us on the road and say, "If you will I can be made clean?"

But must we really ask this question? Don't we already know the wife who is sick and depressed, the daughter who is confused, the worker who is shunned, the mother who sits alone, the street people gathering cans, the adolescent boy despairing of life? We need not look far. The problem is not a lack of needy people around us. The problem is our fear of feeling with them. We fear losing our lives. We fear being swept away. And so, to protect what little stability we have—we too are lepers, after all—we close ourselves up, we try not to feel. Compassion is the enemy of our peace. Yes.

And are we wrong? No, we are not wrong, for this story tells us as well of the cost of compassion, for Jesus and for us. To grasp this, we must read the story in the context of Mark's narrative.

The story is in Mark's first chapter. Jesus has entered the narrative as one who preaches the kingdom of God. His first exorcisms demonstrate that the power of God is stronger than the power of Satan to rule people's lives. But these signs of power have unintended consequences. Jesus suddenly becomes a healer more than preacher. All day long he is closed in the house, healing the sick. His followers cannot even eat. The crowd surrounds the door.

Is this what Jesus wants? Apparently not, for the first chance he gets—at dawn the next morning!—he seeks solitude and plans his escape. When Peter and the others find him and tell him "everyone is seeking you"—obviously to be healed—Jesus turns away. He thinks God has called him to preach. This is how he understands his mission. And he acts on this project. He tells them, "Let us move on to the neighboring villages that I may proclaim the good news there also. That is what I have come to do." He means that preaching, not healing, is his mission.

It is at this very point in his narrative that Mark places the story of the leper. It is as though the leper interrupts Jesus' project—or better, what Jesus thought God's project for him was—with his plea for healing. Here we begin to see the cost of compassion. For Jesus now to enter into this man's need, he must let go of, at least in part, his own project. For him to hear the other as other, feel what he feels, touch him and will what he wills, he cannot stay absolutely on the path that he thought God had chosen for him.

Jesus must die at least a bit to his own vision of his life in order to enter the life of this other. To hear the voice of my lonely, bored, twelve-year-old daughter who wants me to play with her, I must relinquish the absolute hold on me of the televised basketball game. To feel what my distressed wife is feeling, I must let go of my obsessive preoccupation with work and finances. To enter my troubled son's space means leaving the safety of my own. To feel with, suffer with, another, means to suffer as well the loss of at least some part of ourselves.

Precisely here, some ancient New Testament manuscripts reveal, perhaps unintentionally, deep insight into the emotional truth of such loss. Instead of the Greek word found in most manuscripts, *splanknistheis*—he was moved with compassion—these manuscripts have *orgistheis*—he was moved with anger!

How lovely to think of Jesus, like us, angered at this intrusion into his life. How comforting, I think, to know that the Messiah's response of faith had the same cost that you and I experience all the time. Who of us does not know, if we are honest with ourselves, how much anger is generated within us by the demands placed on us by others? This is natural and inevitable. Anger is the healthy response of the living organism to danger and threat. And what is more threatening than to relinquish the part of ourselves that desires, wants, needs? So we feel anger at the lepers in our life who force us to the suffering of compassion. We feel anger as well at the God who teaches us faith through such painful lessons, gives us birth to a new and fuller life through such awful passages of death.

Alas, the story tells us still more about the costs of compassion. At the end of the story there is another exchange between Jesus and the man healed of leprosy. The man who had been isolated and forced to live apart in the desert is now restored to society and can wander the city preaching— the very thing that Jesus had wanted to do! And Jesus? He is forced to stay in the desert, where he cannot preach. He is isolated from his own desire.

And worse: the passage says, "Yet people kept coming to him from every side"—to be healed! Jesus' empathy toward, and healing of, the leper in effect make a leper of him. He is forced into the isolation and loneliness of the helper, the healer.

So can we expect, to the degree that we enter the lives of the needy— that is, each other's lives—that we too will experience the isolation and loneliness that was theirs, so that they can walk freely in the streets of our shared city.

Does this seem unbearably hard? It is the way Jesus went first and the way his Spirit seeks to carve within our freedom. There is this comfort. In Jesus' touch, God reached us. We are, in fact, restored. We can touch others without essential loss. In Jesus' human compassion, God suffered with us, to teach us how. Paul told Timothy, "If we have died with him, we will also live with him" (2 Tim 2:11). How do we die with him? By suffering and dying with and for each other, as he did first for and with us.

LIFE FOR OTHERS[1]

Ezekiel 37:1–14
Acts of the Apostles 4:31–37
John 12:13–28

My sisters in Christ, it is sometimes good to ask this simple question: Why we are doing this and not something else, why we are here and not there?

This evening for example. You could be headed right now for the drag races with a picnic lunch and a tub of beer. You could be sleeping off the final pain of last night's pleasure. You could be sitting with a Diet Coke working on the *New York Times* crossword puzzle: let's see, 1 across, a Sunday evening; 2 down, not in church; 3 across, a happy girl—looking for the clue beneath the clues that makes the puzzle plain.

Instead, we sit together in this space, without benefit of Coca-Cola, spending time working at another sort of word puzzle: let's see: 1 down, Ezekiel 37, dry bones and the big wind; 2 across, Acts 4, possessions laid at the apostles' feet; John 10, a shepherd lays down his life and takes it up again. We sit with these fragments of texts and try to fit them together.

We tell ourselves that we do this not to distract ourselves but to recollect ourselves with God's word. We are here, we say, not to kill time but to sanctify time.

We are thereby exposed as people who live as purposeful schizophrenics. Like the truly mad, we hearken to voices others do not even hear. Unlike the mad, though, we do not thereby withdraw to a private bedlam, but claim to hear rightly the world's true story. Here we bid all flesh keep silence. Here we quiet all the noise of "she said this and I said that, and we

---

1. Sunday service for undergraduate women, Hollins College, Roanoke, Virginia, 1988.

said so and they said thus." We do this so that we can hear the word that we hope can shape our own words into something more than silly chatter.

We puzzle over these texts because in them we hope to find our meaning.

That's at least what we think we ought to say. But let's be honest. A large part of each of us is not here this evening. Part of us is at the drag races, loafing in bed, catching up with laundry, rehearsing the "she said, I said" of Saturday night. We really are schizophrenic, because we each bring at least two minds to this place at once.

And if we are really honest, we can admit that the part of us we dragged violently here by the hair—with all the noise we carried in with us—seems a lot more real and important than this silence. The *New York Times* is a lot more appealing than old Ezekiel and all those bones. The part of us that would rather be over there than here, rather be anywhere but here, squirms under all this holy talk and yells, "Come on, let's go to the drag races!"

Because our minds are so divided, it is even harder for us to grasp the words we hear this evening. Not hard to understand, but hard to accept, for we don't know which words we really want to live by.

From these fragments of texts, a clear-enough pattern emerges. In Ezekiel, the bones in the valley are thoroughly dead, but they are knit together and enlivened by a power not their own. In the Gospel, Jesus identifies himself as one who lays down his life for others, dying so that they may live. In Acts, the first Christians live by the same pattern: possessions, after all, are the symbol of ourselves, and sharing them with others is sharing our life with them, even at the cost of diminishing ourselves.

The pattern, in fact, is strikingly clear. Our real life is a gift given by Another. The logic of gifts is giving. Our life is for others.

It sounds, indeed, like one of those good news, bad news jokes. The good news is that you have been given your life from Another without having done anything to deserve it. The bad news is that you must now give it away.

The problem with this pattern is not a lack of clarity. The problem is that we don't want to hear it. Both the brute facts of our experience and the wisdom of our contemporary world conspire to discredit such a construal of our existence.

The glossy advertisements in high-end magazines convey the same message as do the incessant commercials on television and, for that matter, the typical self-esteem workshop. The old Budweiser ad said it perfectly:

"You only go around once, so you have to grab all the gusto you can!" Other contemporary snippets of wisdom: "Look out for number one!" "You deserve the best!" "You have to help yourself before you can help others!" "Charity begins at home!"

Our age has forgotten every sin but one, which is the failure to be happy, or self-fulfilled. Every discussion must include the language of rights or entitlements and "what's in it for me." Ours is a narcissistic age, pitched to the level of a sustained self-involved whine. Our most emblematic publication is called simply *Self*.

This interpretation of our existence is not simply outside clamor. These are the words that dwell inside us. This is the voice that asks, "Why are you here in this stuffy place, when you could be lolling in bed or drinking beer at the races—as you deserve, have a right to?"

And if that voice speaks to us on this gentle evening, how much louder must it ring in the conflicts and confusions of our everyday life? In the noise of "she said to me and I said to her," how little sense it seems to make to think of life for others. I can barely hold on to what I have! Against the assaults and attacks of people around me, I can barely maintain the fragile walls that I need to make me safe. In the turmoil of multiple rude requests and naked needs, we cling to our life with both hands.

The word spoken by these readings is then a challenge and shock to the voices around us and within us. The message of self-sacrifice and self-disposition for the sake of others threatens the logic of self-preservation. By the measure of MTV and the *New York Times*, we appear foolish when we gather to this word. Worse, we may seem more than a little ludicrous even to ourselves.

As someone who fights in the frightening war of attrition called middle age, I can assure you that the message carried by these readings seems even more foolish when we feel our strength ebbing and our energy slipping away, and when we see the shadow of night creeping across our sunny front porch. When every simple step looks like a cliff-dive, and every simple yes to another seems a spike-wound, the thought that my life is for others seems even more a hopeless ideal or perhaps even a form of delusion.

So I come at last to the real reason we gather as we have this evening. We are not here to celebrate what any one of us has individually accomplished. We cannot claim to act according to this pattern of life for others, only that we are measured by it. Instead, we come to hear the word that does measure us, cleanly and sharply, so we can see how far short we fall.

But even as we do this, together, we come to realize that the real point is not we who are measured, but the One who, with infinite mercy, measures us.

The point is not our solitary lives, but the life of God into which we—together—have been swept up by the mystery of creation, salvation, and sanctification. What we celebrate here is not how we consistently and convincingly give ourselves for each other, but how God has given Godself to us—above all in Jesus, whose entire existence is spelled out by the language of "take, eat, this is my body given for you."

As we celebrate this overwhelming gift of God to us, we also recognize that what each one of us cannot do alone, we are in fact empowered in this place to do together. We have, in truth, each of us left the part of our minds that insists on self-definition and self-determination and self-realization and have come to this place that belongs to no one of us, have come together for the sake of each other, to build up each other, to live for each other, at least during this time. Like the first Christians, we bring our possessions of time and energy and attention to share them with each other and for each other. And by so doing, we may perhaps even feel a small breath moving over our dead bones.

CONFESSING JESUS[1]

Philippians 2:4–21
Mark 8:27–33

My brothers and sisters in Christ, my topic this morning is confessing Jesus. Confessing Jesus is not the same as having an opinion about Jesus. It is rather a matter of conviction and witness, of living our lives in accordance with our profession.

Opinions are easy. Convictions are hard. Opinions require little time or effort to form and demand little involvement of ourselves. Everybody, we like to say, is entitled to an opinion. If that's the case, then opinions are necessarily cheap and easy to come by.

Opinions are what we hear day and night on talk radio and television. Sometimes opinions are uttered by pipe-smoking professors who have written books. Other times by impossibly handsome actors who have made movies. Sometimes opinions are stated in profanity-laced shouting matches—often in shows involving people with more tattoos than teeth. The solemn nattering heard on the panels of experts showcased by CNN and Fox News may have better diction and dentition, but political pundits do not display notably better logic than the yahoos on *The Maury Povich Show*. "Oh well," we mutter, as we listen to such opinion-mongering, "that may be their opinion, but it's not my opinion."

Cheap as they are, opinions rule our spin-happy politics. For more than a few years, the American republic has been directed by popular opinion, checked every day by pollsters as religiously as ancient pagan priests examined the auspices to determine whether the emperor could safely go to war or take a walk. "What's the majority opinion?" That's the key question, that's the basis for steering the ship of state, even if it drives us straight onto the shoals of national disaster.

1. Spartanburg, South Carolina, March 16, 1998.

Ancient philosophers spent a lot of effort trying to distinguish between opinion and truth. They saw that opinions were fickle and untrustworthy precisely because they were so easy to acquire and usually arose from human passions rather than from careful thought or deep commitment. They knew that a state could not be righteous unless it was governed by lovers of wisdom dedicated to the pursuit of truth. Those who ruled by flattering public opinion they called demagogues. The states they led were invariably corrupted from within, leading in turn to the destruction of the populace.

My reason for talking about opinions this morning is not to deliver a lecture on politics, but to suggest that there is an equally great difference between having an opinion about Jesus and confessing Jesus. Having an opinion about Jesus is easy. It requires nothing of us except a willingness to talk. Confessing Jesus is difficult and demands everything of us.

There is a lot of talk and writing these days about Jesus at the level of opinion.[2] Scholars and would-be scholars write books and attend conferences and appear on television debates and talk shows. They express their opinions about Jesus as a historical figure, that is, as a dead man of the past. "I think he was a Jewish peasant who stood for social equality," says Scholar A. "I think he was a guru of a high consciousness," says Scholar B. Scholar C chimes in, "I think he was a prophet opposed to an oppressive temple cult." Scholar D responds, "I think he was an agrarian reformer." At that, Scholar E jumps out of his chair and proclaims, "I think he was a charismatic champion of the politics of compassion rather than the politics of holiness."

Opinions about Jesus are as various as the scholars espousing them. A small industry of Jesus opinion is found in seminars and conferences in which solemn discussion leads to a vote—with the majority opinion deciding—on whether Jesus actually spoke the Lord's Prayer or the parable of the prodigal son. Such debates and elections, publicized by the media, further stir public opinion, as though something more significant was involved beyond opinions of the partially educated about a dead man of the distant past. Influenced by books published by such scholars, in turn, many people in the church turn their dial from one of these opinions to another: "I think that Jesus was . . ."

For those of us who have gathered here this morning in the name of Jesus, however, the operative phrase cannot be "I think that Jesus was"

---

2. The sermon was preached while the "historical Jesus controversy" was still active, and about two years after the publication of my book, *The Real Jesus: The Misguided Quest for the Historical Jesus and the Truth of the Traditional Gospels* (1996).

but, rather, "We confess that Jesus is." We come to this place, not to argue opinions about a dead person of the past but to praise and honor the living Lord Jesus in the present.

Our goal is not to vote on which sayings we think he spoke before his death, but to place our wills in obedience to his voice that continues to speak to us, not only in the pages of Scripture, but also in the stories of our own lives. "We confess with our lips," Paul says in Romans 10:9, "that Jesus is Lord, and we believe in our hearts that God has raised Him from the dead."

If we so confess, and if we so believe, then everything is changed for us, and as the church we stand within our opinion-defined American culture as the most countercultural people imaginable.

Here we cannot operate on the premise that everyone's opinion is as good as anyone else's, for the confession of Jesus is not a matter of opinion. It is a matter of commitment.

If Jesus is not simply a dead person of the past but a presence more powerfully alive today than in first-century Galilee, then our every thought ought to be taken up with seeking his pleasure. What we seek from each other in the church, therefore, is not a better opinion, or even greater knowledge, about the past. What we need from each other is a living witness to the truth of the power of the resurrection in transformed lives, demonstrated by patterns of selfless service and love.

In the body of Christ that is the church, we do not consider the truth that is in Jesus to be one that we make up as we go along, or one that we can cut to our contemporary fashion, or that we can simply observe in others in the way we watch election returns on television. Instead, we confess that the truth of the Lord Jesus that comes to us within the community of faith also summons each one of us to embody and enact this truth by the manner in which we conduct our daily lives.

We do not turn our judgment on the New Testament because its opinions do not match ours. Rather, we consider that the truth by which we live has its irreplaceable witness in Scripture. We do not dismantle the Gospels in order to discover facts about a dead Jesus; we ponder the Gospels in order to learn the living Jesus, "to know," as Paul declares, "the power of the resurrection."

But notice how Paul continues. Notice how coming to know the power of Jesus' resurrection does not make our lives easier—as so much of our society would wish and too much of a watered-down Christianity proposes to offer. Just as the world of advertising pushes medicines for the removal of every pain—the side effects are in the small print—so do many Christian pulpits advertise a Christ who relieves our every suffering. But this is not the truth of the gospel. Paul says that knowing the power of Jesus' resurrection means "a sharing in his sufferings, to be shaped into the form of his death," so that we might also attain resurrection from the dead.

If we take this seriously—and why would we be here this morning if we did not take it seriously?—our opinions about the historical Jesus are irrelevant. What matters is the way our confession of Jesus shapes us into a discipleship of service in the world.

Confessing Jesus means living out, through the power of his Holy Spirit, the pattern of Jesus' life and resurrection. It means being willing to look foolish in order to make others wise, to be weak so that others might be strong, to be poor so that others might be enriched. It means welcoming others as he has welcomed us, bearing one another's burdens as he bore ours, giving our lives to one another in the slow drip of daily devotion as he did for us in his faithful death on the cross.

The way of life demanded by the confession of Jesus makes no sense to a world defined by visible success and easy opinion. Often enough, it also makes little sense to us when we are swamped by the propaganda of that world, which can reduce even our life commitment to the level of just another opinion.

That is why we need to come together as we have this morning, those of us who believe that the point about Jesus is not having opinions about his past, but of showing obedience to him as our Lord in the present. Because we are prone to lose sight of what our commitment truly entails, we need to bear witness to each other concerning the truth that we hear enunciated in this place and nowhere else, that "our citizenship is in heaven, from where we await as well our Savior, the Lord Jesus Christ. He will transform the body of our lowliness. He will conform it to His glorious body. He will do this by the power that enables Him to subdue everything to Himself" (Phil 3:20–21).

May that power of the resurrection touch each of us today. May the amen that we make through Jesus Christ to God our Maker also be the amen that silently shapes our every word and deed in sanctifying service to a suffering world.

THE CHOICE TO RECONCILE[1]

Second Corinthians 5:17–21
Luke 15:1–2, 11–32

My sisters and brothers in Christ, the readings we have just heard read force us, however reluctantly, to think about reconciliation. I say reluctantly, because reconciliation is one of those ideals that we all applaud in the abstract but then resist in our own lives. Mainly, I guess, because it is so hard. Plus, we're not sure we really want to.

The opposite of reconciliation is alienation. We are experts at that. Alienation between nations, fought out in wars. Alienation within nations, expressed by discrimination and oppression. Alienation in small towns, where neighbors cross the street rather than meet. Alienation in big families, where the burdens of hurt given and taken finally gets too great for us to eat together anymore.

Forget for the moment wars between nations and feuds between rivals. We ourselves find all kinds of ways of becoming strangers to each other. There are always good reasons to be alienated from parents, siblings, teachers, priests, neighbors down the street. There is, first of all, the way we have been hurt by each other, followed by the ways our hurt deepens and grows with the nourishment we provide. "I can never forgive my father/ mother/sister/brother/coach/priest, for the way he/she/they did X or Y or Z to me when I was a child/first married/out of a job/grieving. The hurt is still too real, too great, for me to get over it."

Then there are the ways we have simply grown differently and apart. Once we whispered in each other's ears; now we must shout across chasms created by miles, and culture, and education, and money, and power. "I

1. Saint Anthony's Church, Park Falls, Wisconsin, March 22, 1998; with my family, which was experiencing several forms of fissure, in the congregation.

don't understand it," we sometimes say, "we used to be so close; now we can't even talk without getting into a fight. What happened?"

Then there are the ways we have never really felt comfortable with each other because of race, or national heritage, or language, or custom, or appearance, or behavior. "I just don't like being in the same room with someone who looks, talks, smells, dresses, acts, the way she does."

We're experts at alienation. Our world is expert at it and always has been, as history shows us. Start with Cain and move forward. One innovation of our own age is the justification of such alienation. We justify envy based on differences in wealth and social position. We justify rage based on injuries past and present. We justify violence carried out in reaction to racial discrimination. We justify murder in response to religious repression, and do so on the basis of our own religious and national heritage!

That's what we have made of creation from Cain to Khaddafi: a place where differences demand separation, where envy drives competition, and where the logic of competition demands the exclusion or elimination of the other.

But Paul tells us in today's reading from Second Corinthians that if we are in Christ, we are a new creation, one shaped by God's reconciling the world to himself through Christ. How did God do this? In order to accomplish reconciliation, someone has to move. It has to be the stronger one, because the weaker one is not able to move. In Christ, Paul says, God's strength appeared as weakness, God's wisdom appeared as foolishness, God's wealth appeared as poverty. God's life appeared as death, God's righteousness appeared as sin. God in Christ came over to our side to bring us back over to God's side.

The Gospel of Luke, in turn, shows us how God went about reconciling us in Jesus, how he who did not know sin became sin, so that we might in him become God's righteousness.

We see Jesus eating and drinking—that is, sharing in the most basic form of human fellowship—both with the Pharisees who detested him and the sinners and tax collectors who thronged to him. He welcomed all and ate with them.

Jesus is God's body language of reconciliation. He carries children no one else wants in his arms. He embraces the tax collectors who are enemies of the people. He eats and drinks with the disreputable women of the street; he associates with, touches, and is touched by, the sick and the smelly, the confused and the corrupt.

Luke likewise shows us how God's way of reconciling also brings to light the logic of alienation. Jesus' opponents object to his open and indiscriminate embrace of others. They murmur. They complain. They call names: "He eats with tax collectors and sinners." Faced with the option of the new creation that seeks reconciliation between humans, they choose the option of the old creation, seeing the acceptance of others as a rejection of themselves.

So, in response to this attack, Jesus tells three stories. The first two stories are clearly parables about God's reconciling mercy: a man goes out to seek one lost sheep at the risk of losing the ninety-nine and rejoices over its recovery; a woman sweeps her house looking for one lost coin out of ten and rejoices with her friends when she finds it.

It is the last and longest parable, though, that has always fascinated us, because it tells a tale that is so realistic, so profoundly human, that each of us can identify with it in some way. Perhaps through such strong personal identification, we might be drawn into considering the need for reconciliation in our own lives.

Nothing could be more realistic than this story of a divided family. It has more than enough alienation to go around. The thoughtless younger son as much as wishes his father dead when he asks for his inheritance; he abandons the farm work to his older brother; he dissipates all his wealth in a faraway land; then, he comes back home with a clever but implausible cover story.

In the meantime, the father seems to have taken the older son completely for granted, assuming that he understood that "all that I have is yours as long as you are with me" and failing to recognize that well-behaved children also need occasional recognition and thanks.

And the older brother—well, how many of us have not at some point or another identified with the older brother, especially those of us who have always kept the rules and colored within the lines? How, we ask, can this father be so welcoming to a son who has treated him so shabbily, while he has never provided a goat, much less a fatted calf, for his good son to enjoy?

The older son doesn't know if he is more angry at his father or his brother. What he does know is that the last thing he wants is to go from the cold night into that bright place where everyone is singing and laughing as though nothing had happened.

But the father doesn't only search for his careless son and run to welcome him when he straggles up the dusty road. The father also goes out from that warm banquet into the cold night and begs his older son to come in and celebrate with them. It is the older son's choice.

Will he nurture his hurt, the hurt expressed verbally by his distancing language, "this son of yours," or will he receive his father's invitation to join "this brother of yours" within a reconciled family? It is his choice. Luke does not tell us what he chose.

It is also our choice.

THE PIONEER OF FAITH[1]

Genesis 15:1–6
Philippians 3:17—4:1
Luke 13:31–35

My sisters and brothers in Christ, the Letter to the Hebrews—which we did *not* read this morning—calls Jesus the "pioneer and perfecter of faith." It is a fine phrase, but what does it mean? I think it means that when we look at Jesus in the Gospels, we find a human person who went before us on the very path we need to follow. He is, then, our pioneer. And, Jesus did it right. So, he is also the perfecter. And what path did Jesus walk? The walk of faith in God.

When we study Jesus in the Gospels, then, we look to see how he did right—how he did righteously—what we need to do next.

Luke's Gospel, which we *did* read this morning, shows us a Jesus who is a prophet. A prophet is someone who sees the world the way God sees the world and tells other people how to see it that way, too. The prophet Jesus says that the way we run the world is not the way God wants the world to be run. We run the world so that people with money and power and privilege get to be on top and lord it over others. Jesus says this is not the way God sees things.

God wants a world, he says, in which the poor, the outcast, and the weak find a place as important as the rich, the powerful, and the privileged. In fact, Jesus says, God wants to turn the tables by giving the poor, the outcast, and the weak even a higher place in God's eyes. This vision of how the world should run is what Jesus calls God's kingdom. God's kingdom is not one far off in the distance. It is happening now in Jesus' work among ordinary people. He is calling people to join the revolution, to form

1. Redan United Methodist Church, Redan, Georgia, March 11, 2001.

a community that reverses the values the world holds most dear, a community that actually lives by these countercultural values.

In today's reading, Luke depicts Jesus as God's prophet, as he moves on his long journey to Jerusalem. He announces God's rule for the world and invites people to join it. He challenges the crowds surrounding him, he teaches his disciples, he warns those wanting to live by the same old ways.

And because he is a prophet, Jesus also knows that he is in trouble. He knows that the powers in charge won't easily let loose of their privileges. He knows that they resist God's revolution. He knows that they have a history of murdering the prophets who speak for God. And he knows that this journey to Jerusalem will end with his own rejection, torture, and death, at the hands of this world's rulers.

Luke lets us see a small moment in that journey. People pretending to be friends of Jesus warn him away from his path. These Pharisees warn Jesus that the client-king Herod seeks to kill him. Why do I call them pretend friends? Because in Luke's Gospel, the Pharisees always lead the opposition to God's kingdom. They represent the religiously privileged who decide who is in and who is out with God. For some time, in fact, they have been trying to trap Jesus. The very next scene has them watching carefully for a mistake. Precisely because Jesus is popular with sinners and tax collectors (the religiously reprobate), we later learn, the Pharisees grumble and criticize him (Luke 15:1–2).

They also, by the way, are lying about Herod. Herod is certainly interested in seeing Jesus, but even when he later has the chance to put Jesus to death, he does not (23:8–12). So, if the Pharisees are lying and false friends, why do they want Jesus to leave that place? Because they do not want him to bring his revolution to Jerusalem. They don't want to change the way things are done. They don't want to lose their place of privilege. They are quite willing to be the government's stooges if that will do the trick.

Jesus' response proves that he is a prophet and demonstrates his faith. He is a prophet, because he can see them as they really are. He does not flee to safety. He does not say, "Thanks for your help." Instead he tells them, "Go, tell that fox . . ." If they play the king's stooges, let them keep playing the king's stooges. Go tell him for me.

And, he announces *his* intention, which is to keep on doing what he has been doing, proclaiming God's new way of doing things, by healing people and driving out demons. Healing people strengthens them to join the revolution that gathers together all the weak and outcast and poor into a prophetic community. Driving out demons frees people from the chains of spiritual oppression that make them see and use the world in a way that is against God's plan.

Jesus will not stop doing this. Neither false friends nor threats from puppet kings will turn him away. He will, he says, keep going today and tomorrow and the next day. He won't stop until the goal has been reached, even if reaching the goal is through his own death. God's revolution does not depend on Jesus' staying alive by avoiding the agents of the state. God's revolution depends on Jesus being a true prophet even to death at the hands of the state's agents.

Like every prophet, Jesus is human. His steadfastness has a cost. He knows that Jerusalem is the killer of prophets. He aches for his own people's acceptance of God's message. His compassion is like that of the hen seeking to protect her chicks by gathering them to herself (13:34). But he cannot force them to accept God's revolution. And he knows that their rejection of God's revolution means also their rejection of him, even if that rejection will leave their own house being left empty and abandoned (13:35).

But even in the face of this, he clings to the promise of Scripture, which declares of the Messiah, "Blessed is He who comes in the name of the Lord." Jesus is quoting from Psalm 118:26. This is the song that will be sung when he finally enters the city (Luke 19:38). Just before the line Jesus quotes, the psalm says, "The stone which the builders rejected, this has become the cornerstone. The Lord has done this and it is marvelous in our eyes" (Ps 118:22–23). Jesus is the stone rejected by the builders. He is also the cornerstone that God uses to build a people shaped according to Jesus' vision.

What do we learn about our own faith from the faith of Jesus? We learn that it must be fearless in the face of opposition and distortion, that it must face the real possibility of rejection, that it must embrace an inclusive compassion even for those who reject it, that it must lean on the truth of Scripture that God works triumph even out of human tragedy. Most of all, we learn that faith continues in every circumstance to cast out the demons holding people captive and to heal the illnesses that keep people from full participation in God's revolution. That, in short, faith keeps on keeping on.

We also heard this morning a reading from Saint Paul's letter to the Philippians. Paul, as we know, never narrates the story of the prophet Jesus. Paul's concern is always how Jesus' story gets retold in the lives of his readers.

The believers in Philippi did not have to deal with the Pharisees or with King Herod. Their circumstances were completely different. But the faith of Jesus could still be their faith.

That's what it means to be a resurrection people: that the life of Jesus can be written again and again in the hearts of humans all over the world and in every age by the power of the Holy Spirit. Because we have been gifted with the Holy Spirit, we can be faithful as Jesus is faithful. We can't go back and walk on the same ground he did. But we can go forward, walking in the footsteps of his faith (see 1 Pet 2:21).

The Philippian church was distracted from its faithful following of Jesus by attitudes of rivalry and envy (Phil 1:15). Some members of the community wanted more status than others. They competed with each other, looking to their own interests rather than the interests of the group as a whole.

They were in real danger of losing the vision of the prophet Jesus, whose revolution means that all seek the good of the other. This is the mind of Christ that Paul teaches them over and over. He reminds them that Jesus did not seek his own good, but gave up all of his own status—as God's equal!—in his faithful obedience.

Paul knows that God's revolution is difficult. It goes against the grain of how the world usually works. The world runs by the rules of those who look to earthly things (as Paul calls them) rather than heavenly things. And the world feeds those who treat their bellies as their god.

So, Paul asks his readers to learn revolutionary faith from the people who already live in the way Jesus lived, that is, who give up their own power and possessions and privilege, so that the weak can get stronger, the poor can get richer, and the outcast can find a home.

Paul reminds them of how he himself gave up his power and possessions and privilege as a Pharisee, in order to join Jesus' revolution by faith. He reminds them of their friends Timothy and Epaphroditus, who cared about the Philippians' needs much more than their own. Imitate such people, Paul says, live like them.

My sisters and brothers in Christ, if our citizenship really is in heaven, then let's act like foreign agents who are trying to bring about a revolution here below. Let's seek to live by the radical standard of the faith of Jesus Christ. And let us learn that standard from the witness of the saints who live among us.

MIRACLES AND US[1]

Exodus 24:12–18
Second Peter 1:16–21
Matthew 17:1–8

My brothers and sisters in Christ, the lectionary readings this morning are bound to give us a religious inferiority complex. Why can't we have experiences of God like those reported so confidently in the Bible?

Moses goes up on the mountain, we are told, because he is summoned directly by the Lord God: "Come up to me on the mountain, and I will give you the tablets of stone with the law and the commandment, which I have written for their instruction." Moses goes up, and the cloud covers the mountain for six days. The cloud is the glory—or presence—of the Lord. On the seventh day, the Lord calls Moses, and he climbs still higher on the mountain. He enters into the cloud, with its devouring fire, on the top of the mountain. He stays there forty days in the presence of God. And he comes down from the mountain with the tablets of the law written by God's own finger. Now *this* is what we call a theophany! Here are God and a human being like us, joined in close consultation, while all around them, fireworks signal that something really big is happening.

But why do such things happen only to people in the Bible and not to us in our pew?

The author of the Second Letter of Peter gives, if anything, an even more dramatic report, this time not about an encounter with God long ago and far away, but in his own lifetime. He and those with him—he uses the pronoun *we*—were eyewitnesses of Jesus' majesty as seen on the holy mountain. They heard the voice that said, "This is my son, the beloved, with whom I am well pleased." In this experience, Peter said, they had the message of the prophets confirmed. They knew that they were not involved

1. Trinity Lutheran Church, Sacramento, California, February 10, 2002.

with clever myths, but with truth. In the same way that the prophets had truly been "moved by the Holy Spirit and spoke from God," so was the vision of majesty and the hearing of God's voice a matter of fact and not fiction.

Finally, we have heard this morning the evangelist Matthew's recital of Jesus' transfiguration before Peter, James, and John, once more on a high mountain. Once more also, there is the palpable presence of the divine: the dazzling light, the cloud, the voice, even the prophetic figures of Moses and Elijah standing with Jesus. The disciples not only see Jesus shot through with God's glory, they hear God's own voice declaring Jesus to be the beloved son in whom God is pleased.

Now, if you and I have not been experiencing God like this, we must conclude that we are either in the wrong place or in the wrong time. Either we are too seldom on high mountains in the Middle East, or we have the misfortune of being born outside Bible time.

I speak lightly. But I have a serious point. When reading or hearing Scripture, we cannot help wondering at the gap between the revelations of God it so regularly reports and the singular lack of such revelations in your world and mine.

This disparity has from the time of the European Enlightenment given the cultured despisers of Christianity just the ammunition they needed to discredit both the Bible and the contemporary claim to miracles.

"Show me one happening now," they said, "and we will take you more seriously." They didn't mean some subtle healing or spiritual transformation, but a genuine, twenty-one-gun-salute-type revelation, a mountaintop with-fireworks-and-flame-type revelation. "Show me," they say, "a visible, self-validating, caught on the radar screen, detectable at least by mass spectrometry-type revelation. You don't have any to display? Case closed." Thus, they conclude that biblical revelation is a fairy tale for grown-ups, a Never-Neverland for the distraction of people for whom the everyday world is too much reality to bear.

Even if we do not hold these views, they affect us. We can hardly help wondering ourselves at the apparent contrast between the way God acts so powerfully and palpably in the Bible and the way God fails to act that way in our neighborhood.

Perhaps a way we can begin to think about this is to reconsider our premise that the Bible simply reports revelation, as though God's self-revelation occurs the way car accidents occur and the Bible is like a newspaper that reports accidents. Maybe it would be more helpful if we thought of the Bible less as reporting revelation and more as participating in revelation.

Here's what I mean. Let us suppose for the moment that God, as the One who creates the world new at every moment, as the One who calls into being at every second that which is not, the One who is the invisible presence behind every coming into being that we call the world, let us suppose that this God acts in and upon the world now as he did then, and therefore also then as he does now.

Let us suppose, in other words, that Moses did *not* encounter God on the mountain as though he was entering a volcanic eruption. Let us imagine that the mountaintop, clouds, and fire were the symbols used to express the way in which Moses did discern the claims of God upon God's world, a discernment that led to the law inscribed on tablets. Let us imagine that this discernment was so new in the world, so powerful a perception into the truth of the world, so potent an agency for reconstructing the world, that it could truly be thought of as a word from heaven, as God's word.

Moses was God's prophet because Moses had ears with which to hear the cries of the oppressed slaves in Egypt that no one else seemed to hear. Moses heard the word God wanted to express about the way stealing and oppression and deceit destroy the harmony of God's world and destroy the image of God that is stamped on the body of slaves as well as of masters.

Moses was God's prophet because he had eyes to see what others failed to see. He saw in the stooped backs of forced laborers and in the towering arrogance of the pyramids the twinned offspring of the human impulse toward idolatry, he saw what follows from having other gods preferred to the One who creates the world at every moment and calls humans out of the Egypt of oppression in every season.

The biblical narrative about Moses uses all the symbolism available to express how, in this prophet's words, God was getting through to humans. Thus the mountaintop, traditional site of meetings between gods and humans. Thus the clouds and fire, signs of the presence of the divine. The biblical text participates in revelation precisely by showing, in hindsight, the deepest meaning of events which in their occurrence may well have been on a flat plain, in the sunshine, and in absolute quiet.

The Gospel and Letter of Peter likewise report as a single event of visible transfiguration the perception by the disciples of who Jesus was even during his human ministry.

Was this, in fact, a single, momentary event? Did it happen on a mountain? Were Moses and Elijah standing there physically with Jesus? Was there a cloud that covered the disciples, radiant clothing, a voice from heaven?

It is no accident that the transfiguration is described in terms that unmistakably recall Moses' encounter with God on Mount Sinai, or that Moses is here shown with Elijah—another mountain man—testifying to Jesus. The Gospel writers used these symbols deliberately to evoke the resonances of God's earlier prophets. They intended to tell us, their readers, the truth that even Jesus' closest followers could not really grasp until after his resurrection: that he is God's beloved Son, to whom we are uniquely to listen.

These descriptions of Jesus' transfiguration participate in revelation rather than simply report it. The transfiguration account uses the symbols of God's revealing activity to disclose the deeper dimensions of the humanity of Jesus.

Please note that I am by no means suggesting that there is no event or no experience on which these revelatory accounts are based. Just the opposite. I am convinced there is. I am convinced that the law of Moses is literally unthinkable if Moses did not hear and see from God what other humans had never before heard or seen so clearly or so well. Such prophetic insight is no less an experience or event, no less real if happening in solitude and quiet rather than in mountain pyrotechnics.

Similarly, I absolutely believe Peter when he says that belief in Jesus is not based on humanly constructed myths but on actual human experience, and that people who followed Jesus did see in him more than what was normally human and, after the experience of receiving his resurrection Spirit, did, in fact, perceive him as transfigured in the fullest sense of the term, since in the fullest sense of the term Jesus was now the Son who shared completely in the life and glory of God.

But such experiences and insights need not have happened in a single transfixing moment. They may have occurred—indeed, I am suggesting that they did occur—in ways that are closer to our own experience. The biblical writers, however, shape those experiences and insights into narratives that disclose the truth within them. And in stories, this can only be done with bells and whistles, or clouds and flames.

I am not, in short, suggesting that God did not reveal Godself through Moses and Jesus. I am suggesting that the biblical accounts might lead us to think that such revelation happened only in extraordinary ways.

More important, I suggest that God continues to reveal just as truly and powerfully in our world today. God is the living God. The same God who created in the beginning continues to create now. The same God who spoke through Moses speaks through prophets today. The same God who acted through Jesus in his deeds of liberation and healing continues to act today in deeds of liberation and healing. Because of the resurrection, indeed, the Holy Spirit of Jesus is present within and among us.

Each body we meet bears the potential of revealing the living Christ. In every voice we hear, we can discern God's word. In every human person, we can detect the writing by God's finger.

The question for us, I think, is: How we can participate in revelation today? How can we, like Moses, see and hear in the patterns of political and economic life the destructive idolatries that cry out for God's justice? How can we detect in the twisted faces of the addicted and the addled the contorting effects of our deranged culture? And how can we hear and see the word of God that is addressed to us in such circumstances?

Likewise, how can we, like Peter and John and James, perceive the face of Christ in our world? How can we see and hear the presence of the risen One in the little ones today, the strangers and enemies who challenge us, the families who irritate us, the saints who inspire us?

You and I can begin by reading Scripture not as the report of revelations no longer available to us, but as a script that teaches us the symbols through which we can see and hear things we otherwise would not, beneath and within the surface play of social systems and human freedom. And by so reading Scripture, we will learn better how to read our own lives, not as the tedious repetition of old things, but as the surprising revelation of the always-new God.

PAUL AND THE STORY OF JESUS[1]

Philippians 2:1–14

My brothers and sisters in Christ, one of the constant complaints about the apostle Paul is that he talks too little about the human Jesus. It is true that just about every other sentence in his letters has the phrase "our Lord Jesus Christ," but when he uses that phrase, he refers to the resurrected One who is powerfully present among Paul's readers through the Holy Spirit.

What about the humanity of Jesus? Many readers find little evidence in his letters that Paul thought it important, and some suggest that Paul either ignored or even slighted the human Jesus. Recently, various questers of the historical Jesus have sharpened the complaint. They say that Paul simultaneously invented Christianity and destroyed the Jesus movement.

But their complaint is wrong. The truth is that, for Paul, the humanity of Jesus is of great, even central, importance.

Granted, Paul tells none of the short stories reported in the Gospels about Jesus' actions. And Paul seldom quotes Jesus' sayings. When he does quote them, though, Jesus' words are authoritative, as in the matters of divorce or the support of ministers. Most noteworthy, Paul quotes the words Jesus said to his disciples at his final meal with them, when he interpreted the bread and wine as his body and blood. But if one thinks only of Jesus' actions and words, perhaps it is accurate to say that the human Jesus does not much appear in Paul's letters.

But if not in words or deeds, how could Jesus' humanity appear in them?

What is important about the human Jesus for Paul is not this or that thing he did, this or that thing he said, but the story of the way he lived his life and the way he died. I don't mean by Jesus' story here a set of facts,

---

1. Independent Presbyterian Church, Birmingham, Alabama, September 29, 2002.

although when we look closely, we see that Paul actually reports more of the basic facts of Jesus' story than we might have expected. No, I mean instead the story of Jesus as the depiction of his human character. For Paul, Jesus is important for the way he was human, and that way of being human is important because that is the way we are meant to be human as well.

Paul knows that the life Jesus lived as a first-century Palestinian Jew stays in the past. It is impossible for others to repeat or even imitate the singular historical path of Jesus. Jesus is not significant for others—for us!—because he is a male, or Jewish, or wore a robe and sandals, or came from Galilee, or taught in parables. All that belonged only to Jesus. It is nontransferable.

Paul's great insight into the power and presence of the Holy Spirit that came on believers as a result of Jesus' resurrection is that this Spirit could shape other people's character into Jesus' own, so that they could truly live "in him" and he could really live "in them." The work of the Holy Spirit, for Paul, is to replicate in the freedom of others the faith of Jesus.

What is this faith of Jesus? It is his absolute trust and obedience toward God at every moment of his life, his refusal to be measured by any other measure or answerable to any other loyalty. So much are faith and obedience linked, for Paul, that he speaks in Romans of "the obedience of faith" (1:5; 16:25), and can speak of Jesus' response to God in Romans 3:21–26 in terms of faith, and of the same response two chapters later in terms of obedience (5:12–21).

How was this trust and obedience of Jesus—his faith in God—expressed? In his willingness at every moment to give himself in service to those around him, giving his body for them and his blood for them, not only at the moment of his death, but through all his life. Jesus, says Paul in Galatians 2:20, is the One who "loved me and gave himself for me." This constitutes the fundamental story of Jesus, a story at whose heart is not plot, but character.

And as such, it is a story into which others can be grafted, that others can live out in the circumstances of their own lives according to the same pattern. This is in fact what Paul means when he tells the Galatian churches, "If we live by the Spirit, we should walk by the Spirit" (Gal 5:25) and spells out this walking a few verses later: "Bear one another's burdens and so fulfill the pattern of the Messiah" (6:2). Similarly, Paul tells the Romans that they should be transformed by the renewal of their mind (Rom 12:1–2) and follows this with "put on the Lord Jesus Christ" (13:14). And he reminds the Corinthian believers that they have not received the spirit of the world, but the Spirit that comes from God (1 Cor 2:12), and follows that by stating "we have the mind of Christ" (2:16).

We have heard very similar words in our reading from Philippians this morning. After talking about the Spirit's work in the community (Phil 2:1–4), Paul says, "Have this mind in you which was also in Christ Jesus" (2:5). Actually, the Greek is closer to this: "Think this way among you, that was also in Christ Jesus." Paul wants them to think and make decisions (the Greek *phronein* means making prudential judgments) among themselves in a manner conformed to Christ's own.

Then Paul reminds them of what this way of thinking is by telling the story that we call the Christ hymn in 2:6–11 and concludes with an exhortation to continue in this kind of faithful obedience. It is a famous and well-loved passage. I will not tell you anything about it this morning that you don't already know. But even the reminder of intimately loved ones can help us appreciate them more. What I want us to appreciate most of all this morning is the way Paul connects the story of Jesus and the life of faith within the Philippian community.

We call Philippians 2:6–11 a hymn, but it is also clearly a story about Jesus. Some scholars think that the first part of it is about the incarnation; "being in the form of God he emptied himself and took the form of a slave" is read in terms of the divine word taking on the human condition. That understanding is certainly possible, although the rest certainly focuses on Jesus "becoming in the likeness of humans and found in form as a human being." Other scholars today read the entire passage as about Jesus in his humanity. If we so read it as a story about the human Jesus, then Paul invites us to consider it as a story of Jesus' character: how Jesus reckoned things, how he made decisions.

The basic movement of the story from divine status (in the form of God) to the lowest of human conditions (form of a slave), and then a return to the highest status of all, as Lord before whom all must bend the knee, is clear enough. But Paul shows us the inside of this progression. The final stage is one God accomplishes, not Jesus: "God highly exalted him and gave him a name above every other name."

All the earlier stages, however, result from Jesus' own decision, his way of thinking or reckoning. Paul tells us that though he was in the form of God, "he did not consider equality of God something to be seized [or grasped]." Here we have a reckoning—"he did not consider"—and an evaluation—"equality with God is not to be seized." As a result of that reckoning and evaluation, Jesus "empties himself out, taking the form of a slave." He empties himself of what could have been his fullness.

Then, Paul tells us, when he is in the form of a human being, he "lowers himself," accomplishing this lowering by means of his obedience, that is, his faithful hearing of, and trust in, God. He does this so absolutely that he can legitimately be seen "in the form of a slave." He does it so fully that it leads to his death. He does this so unreservedly that he embraces the shame of death on a cross. Here we see the faith of Jesus as obedience, and the death of Jesus as the body language of his service as a slave. In Jesus' decisions, his reckonings, we find the character of the human being Jesus as one of radical obedience toward God and service to others as a slave.

But how does Paul connect Jesus' way of thinking, Jesus' character, to the Philippians?

The thing that strikes us first is that Paul addresses his readers as a group. He is not advocating for a set of dispositions that only one person should have, or that a small cadre should have. Paul aims at a mindset that should be present in every member of the community. He says, think this way "among you." The faith of Jesus is not just what's in our individual hearts; it's how we live together.

The second thing we notice is Paul's language in 2:1–2, where he summons the Philippians to such a shared commitment. What does he say should manifest their "fellowship in the Spirit," their "encouragement in Christ," their "consolation in love?" It is, he says, that they all share the same outlook, the same way of thinking about things, the same way of making decisions within the community.

Paul here links the Greek word for fellowship (*koinonia*) to the attitudes characterizing close friends in the ancient world. Friends, it was said, shared all things, had one soul, thought the same way. Thus, for the Greeks, friendship meant a fellowship in which all shared all that they were and had.

For ancient thinkers, the opposite of such friendship was the vice of envy. Envy generates rivalry and conflict, because envy seeks what the other has and is willing to seize it by force. We should not be surprised that Paul here pushes for a form of friendship, since as he noted early in the letter, some of them even preach Christ out of envy and rivalry (1:15).

But Paul does not simply oppose friendship to envy. The fellowship of the Philippians is of the Spirit, and it gives encouragement in Christ, and it leads to love. Nevertheless, look at how he asks them to think: "Be of the same mind, have the same love, be of full accord. Have one mind."

What does it mean for an entire community to have the same mind as an expression of the Holy Spirit, as a manifestation of love? Does Paul mean that in a church as diverse as this one—and all churches are diverse to some degree—everyone should have the same opinion about everything, have exactly the same perspective on affairs, look at things in exactly the same way? Does Paul suggest that fellowship in the Spirit means conformity, or that unity in the Spirit demands uniformity? Does having the mind of Christ make us march in lockstep?

I think not. I think, in fact, that Paul means just the opposite. He wants them to be different in their respective perspectives and personal projects. Indeed, true unity is only possible when people are different as much as they are alike. But in the context of their life together, Paul wants all of them to pursue their personal projects in a certain way, namely with the mind of Christ. This is the "one mind" Paul wants each of them to employ in their decisions. They are to have Christ's mind, that is, view things the way Jesus viewed them.

What does this mean in the concrete? In 2:3–4, Paul provides an invaluable insight into the dynamics of faith within a community. He shows us what it means to seek to be obedient together, to think together with the mind of Christ. He spells out how to do it.

He begins with the negative. He tells them not to act out of selfish ambition or conceit. Here he evokes the dispositions of people driven by rivalry and envy. They want what they want, and at any cost to others. They want higher status and are willing to seize it. They plow ahead with their personal ambitions, no matter how they affect others. It is all about them. And if every member of a community thinks this way, the community does not long remain one. Worship becomes fractious, meetings fall apart, relationships become competitions. Fellowship in the Spirit is lost because the mind of Christ is lost.

Paul then describes positively what living by the mind of Christ means. Notice that he uses the same terms here that he will use to describe Jesus. Jesus did not reckon equality with God as something to be seized. Jesus lowered himself in humility. So are the Philippians—and we—to reckon with humility. Paul draws the Philippians—and us—into the very story of Jesus in describing the way believers are to act in the community. He is making the mind of Christ the measure of how we think when we are with each other.

And Paul gets even more specific. Let each one, he says—note that, this is a mind each one of us needs to live by—let each one pay attention not only to one's own things, but also the things of others. This is a shift in consciousness from selfishness and solipsism to the awareness of community. There are other interests in the room besides my own! Other people see things differently than I do! They seek different goals. I have a project, but they have projects as well. And if we are to live together in the fellowship of the Spirit rather than as a fractured assembly, then we need—each one of us—to learn to think in a new way.

Not in the way the world in its propaganda encourages us to think: "You deserve it, you are entitled, fulfill your needs, it's all about you"—as though we were lords and ladies deserving service. No, we need to think in the way shown us by the story of Jesus, the way in which he showed us how to be faithful precisely in the manner of a slave, whose very existence is defined in terms of the interests of others always coming first.

The story of Jesus by which Paul wants us to measure our own stories is not an easy one. It is demanding. Faith is not simply a matter of believing in things that don't necessarily impact my ways of acting. Nor is faith simply a matter of my internal piety or virtue. Faith, Paul tells us, is the hard business of living together in this world, in this church.

Thinking with the mind of Christ is so hard because it goes so directly against our natural grain. How difficult it is to truly obey and truly serve in the manner shown us by Christ. Paul states that each one of us must have a real project and also be willing to forego our project for the sake of the larger good. This is authentic faith. This is also living in constant stress, constant attentiveness. It means that we must pay attention both to what we want and what others around us want.

This is a painful sort of attentiveness. It is much easier for me simply to be willful. I know what I want, and I ignore you completely. I want what I want; who cares what you want? Most of us recognize this disposition as something other than the obedience of faith! But some of us fall into the error of supposing the opposite of willfulness to be authentic faith, namely willessness. Whatever you want, I will go along with. I won't let myself want anything. I will refuse to form a project of my own. But this isn't genuine faith, either. It is a distortion of faith. It would have been meaningless for Jesus to empty himself, after all, if there had not been a fullness that could be emptied out. No, the faith of Jesus calls us into the complexity of life together and demands that each of us be attentive not only to each other but also to ourselves, not only ourselves but also to others.

Because this is such a difficult way to think, such a difficult story to live, we all tend to avoid it. We need to be reminded of how our story is to be shaped by the story of Jesus. We need to be strengthened in our minds by the mind of Christ. We need to learn from each other slowly and with patience what it means to live out the obedience of faith, in the power of the Holy Spirit. Paul reminds us that although this process is very much one of our moral striving, we "work out [our] own salvation in fear and trembling" and that it is always and above all God's own project for us; Paul says, "It is God who is at work in you, enabling you both to will and to work for his good pleasure" (2:12–13).

SOME HARD TRUTHS[1]

John 15:1–8

My brothers and sisters in Christ, some passages of Scripture—like this one about the vine and the branches from Jesus' farewell speech in John's Gospel—are so familiar that we don't really hear them. The words lull us. We relax. We have heard them so many times, we can almost lip-sync with the lector. We slip into the comfortable sofa of ritual reassurance, fully confident that nothing disturbing will occur.

Nothing so very tragic about this. Indeed, there is much to be said for the power of Scripture to console. And, for that matter, much to be said for familiar ritual. Life outside these walls is chaotic and scary. A little slice of beauty, a small scrap of comfort, a bit of predictable assurance, is not altogether bad. To hear about remaining—or even resting—in the life-giving vine that is Jesus is to have an appropriate sabbath. To be told that whatever we ask for as we rest in him will be given is to receive a powerful sabbath promise.

But still, there is some loss when Scripture speaks only comfort and not also challenge. For those of us who are cradle Catholics, in fact, it is difficult to hear these words in any other way than as comforting.

One of the gifts brought us by new converts to the church is regaining some sense of the shock and surprise that Jesus' words convey when they are heard fresh. The amazement of newcomers at Jesus' words remind us of how Christianity revealed to the world not only a completely unexpected Savior—a lowly Jewish teacher who was executed under state authority—but revealed as well, in the words and the deeds of that Savior, a completely unexpected view of the world and way of living in the world.

Those of us who have become completely acculturated Christians need especially to hear Jesus' words in all their prophetic power. What do

1. Saint Pius X Parish, San Diego, California, May 18, 2003.

111

I mean by acculturated Christians? I mean those of us who have forgotten that being a Christian is not just another interesting version of American citizenship but is, in fact, at the core, a challenge to contemporary American culture. I mean those of us who have become so accustomed to the world in which we spend every hour of the week—except for this one hour set aside for worship—that we have forgotten that the truths we celebrate here are not only different from the ones celebrated by that daily world, but also, if we took them seriously, stand against that everyday, workaday world in fundamental ways. Allow me to suggest three for your reflection.

First, as we all know, nothing is more American than rugged individualism. We each stand on our own feet. We make it on our own. We are self-reliant. We are independent. Or so goes the story we tell ourselves. We define our liberty as a freedom from entanglement, a freedom to pursue our own goals without reference to others. Our individualism has become so pronounced, in fact, that we increasingly live in separate and closed-off enclaves, distanced from our families and strangers to our neighbors. We increasingly become a society that is tenuously linked by the internet in that weird combination of seclusion and voyeurism we call virtual reality. And increasingly, we die in the way we have lived, apart and alone.

The reading from John about the vine and the branches disputes this entire view of things. True life is not independence from others and individual striving. It is a matter of deep mutual dependence and interdependence. Jesus is utterly dependent on the God who gives him life. And we live because we are the branches of the vine that is Jesus. We depend on his life for our life. And more, we are all branches of that one vine, meaning that our lives are linked and interdependent, so that we flourish or fail together. The Gospel tells us that full humanity is not found in the singular genius or the bold adventurer who conquers all in solitude, but is found in the community of solidarity into which God has invited us through the death and resurrection of Jesus and the gift of the Holy Spirit that binds us together.

Second, as Americans, we love to proclaim the virtues of capitalism. We praise the free market. We wish all the world's peoples could abandon their infatuation with socialism and join in the free-enterprise system. We never give any thought to the fact that capitalism has at its root the logic of envy. The logic of envy equates being and worth with having, with possessing. To have more is to be more. When you own more than me, I am grieved, for that implies you are more, are worth more, than me. I am diminished when you increase. In a universe of limited resources, then, our competition is real and even lethal. Success is measured by the number and cost of things we acquire. We are consequently all constant accountants, checking our piles of possessions with alternating smugness and panic. It may be money, it may be houses or boats, it may be books, or acquaintances, or contacts, or friends, or ideas, or projects of any sort. The point is, we keep score. They all can be piled up and counted; and when counted, they signal our success. The one who dies with the most toys, as the T-shirt has it, wins.

But this passage from John's Gospel tells us something quite different. It says that human life is not about a success that can be measured by possessions outside of us, but, rather, about a fruitfulness that is the maturing of life within and around us. Life is not a matter of beating out others. It is a matter of making others stronger and more alive because they are joined to us. Fruit is the mature expression of the plant. It is not something that the plant buys or acquires, but is the full expression of the plant's very being. When we bear fruit as the vine of the Lord, then we grow within the life that God has given us and we give life to others as well. The measure of our maturity, therefore, is not how much we have, but is who we are and, even more, who others can be because we are with them. So we are to ask: Is the life of others better and richer because we are with them, or is it diminished and shrunken?

Third, as Americans we are dedicated in principle to the pursuit of happiness. But in our contemporary culture, happiness has increasingly been identified as pleasure, so our dedication is to the pursuit of pleasure and the avoidance of pain. As a result, we are, without question, the most addicted population that has ever inhabited the planet. We are addicted to more drugs than we can possibly outlaw; we are addicted to drink, to gambling, to sex, to acquisition, to performance, to entertainment. Our lives are a restless round of distraction and avoidance. We even raise our children with the premise that they should never have to suffer hard things, even as we commit them from the time they are toddlers to the addictive work ethic of capitalism in schooling and in sports. It is even possible today to buy into—I use the phrase advisedly—forms of Christianity that avoid any mention of the cross of Jesus, even find the symbol of the cross offensive, and promise success and prosperity as the payoff for the investment of faith.

Jesus, however, speaks in today's reading of the cutting and pruning of the vine even when it is fruitful, so that it can bear even more fruit. He reminds us with these words that all real growth in living things requires pain and suffering. As body-cultists, we appear to understand this when we declare "no pain, no gain." But what applies to the stretching and growth of muscles applies to all forms of life, physical, emotional, mental, and spiritual. Life grows through suffering. It is pain, rather than pleasure, that makes us larger. I don't mean pain sought for its own sake; otherwise, dropping a barbell on your feet would be as useful as lifting it over your head. No, I mean the pain that accompanies growth into a larger life. We can't get smarter without the pain of stretching our minds around new and threatening truths. We cannot grow emotionally without stretching our hearts around new and frightening experiences, some of which hurt more than we can say. And we cannot grow into the full presence of God without the pain of letting go our small pieties and the pleasure of certainty, and stepping into the larger, and more frightening, world into which God invites us.

When a plant is pruned, there is the experience of death for the sake of new life. When God prunes us, it feels like death. Indeed, we can scarcely tell whether we are the branches that are being cut away because they are unfruitful, or we are branches being pruned to become more fruitful. In our actual experience, both forms of cutting seem like death. How can we tell if it is God at work? We can tell by the greater life in the vine, by the way in which those to whom we are joined grow and reach a fuller form of life.

The good news from God in Jesus Christ is not the same as the Declaration of Independence of the United States of America. Good Christians can be good American citizens. But being a good Christian is not the same thing as being a good American citizen. The Gospel passage we have heard today reminds us of why this is so. It challenges us to consider the ways we need, each of us, to think through the view of the world, and of our being in the world, that is demanded of us as followers of Jesus Christ.

A LARGE-ENOUGH FAITH[1]

Luke 17:5–10

My sisters and brothers in Christ, not everything that the Gospels report Jesus saying makes a lot of sense. Such is the case with the first words that Jesus declares in today's reading from Luke's Gospel. The disciples are on the road with Jesus as he makes his way to Jerusalem. They say to him, "Increase our faith," meaning, "Make it larger." Jesus' answer seems oddly nonresponsive. Instead of saying "here's how to enlarge your faith," he appears to suggest either that they have *no* faith, or that the faith they already have should be enough for them, or both at the same time. He says, "If you have faith the size of a mustard seed, you would say to this mulberry tree, 'Be uprooted and planted in the sea,' and it would obey you." Uprooted by a human word? *Planted* in the sea? Jesus' words compound improbabilities and seem neither clear nor particularly instructive.

The three versions of this saying suggest that the evangelists also were not entirely sure exactly what Jesus had said or what it meant. The earliest version is in Mark 11:23–25. There it occurs when Jesus demonstrates his own power by withering a fig tree and tells his disciples, "Have faith in God. Amen, I say to you, whoever says to this mountain, 'Be lifted up and thrown in the sea,' and does not doubt in his heart but believes that what he says will happen, it shall be done for him. Therefore, I tell you, all that you ask for in prayer, believe that you will receive it and it shall be yours." Mark's version is even more extravagant—throwing a mountain into the sea—but it is clearer. Mark connects such powerful faith to the power of prayer. Prayer is the instrument that works wonders.

Matthew likes the saying so much that he uses it twice. The first time, it follows another miracle of Jesus, the healing of the boy possessed by a demon. The disciples want to know why they couldn't do the same. Jesus

1. Akron, Ohio, October 3, 2004.

answers, "Because of your little faith. Amen, I say to you, if you have faith the size of a mustard seed, you will say to this mountain, 'Move from here to there,' and it will move. Nothing will be impossible for you" (Matt 17:20). Again, the mountain. Not thrown into the sea, but still, moved by human faith. Like Mark, Matthew also has the saying in connection with Jesus' withering of the fig tree and makes it a lesson on prayer: "Amen, I say to you, if you have faith and do not waver, not only will you do what has been done to the fig tree, but even if you say to this mountain, 'be lifted up and thrown into the sea,' it will be done. Whatever you ask for in faith, you will receive" (Matt 21:21).

You will notice that it is not Luke's relatively more modest version of uprooting a mulberry tree and planting it in the ocean that captured the imagination of later Christians—though it is certainly spectacular enough—but the more extravagant versions found in Matthew and Mark, which have mountains thrown into the sea. Also standard in the Christian tradition was the connection that Matthew and Mark had Jesus draw between this miraculous outcome and the practice of confident prayer.

And once the saying floated free from the context of the Gospel narratives, it began to work great mischief among followers of Jesus. It worked this mischief by suggesting a cause-and-effect relationship between faith or prayer and the performance of remarkable deeds. Believe hard enough, people came to think, and you can command mountains to move, and they will. Pray hard enough, children were taught, and you can heal an epileptic child or wither a fig tree.

The equation did the greatest mischief when it was used to support the claims of faith healers and their clients. If the healing does not happen, the fault is the lack of faith—not the faith of the healer, to be sure, but the faith of the client. There is no need here to fixate on the charlatanism of televangelists. Many of us know, much closer to home, how the chronically ill among us have added the insult of guilt to the injury of their illness, by blaming themselves for their failure to improve. "If only I had enough faith, if only I prayed more fervently, I would not remain such a burden on my family and friends." Others of us have applied the equation at times of crisis in our lives: "If only we had prayed more faithfully, our beloved mother would not have suffered so at the end, or our adolescent boy would not have run the car off the highway, or our darling infant would not have died in her crib." We lacerate ourselves with blame, multiplying the devastating effect of life's sorrows.

The same equation has also, infamously, given Christianity's crit-
ics one of their more reliable arguments against what they regard as the
fatuousness of faith. The sheer grandiosity of Jesus' statement suggests, in
their eyes, being out of touch with reality. Has anyone ever seen a mountain
moved or thrown into the sea? Or, as David Hume skeptically asked, has
anyone actually seen an epileptic healed simply by someone's prayer?

We all know firsthand accounts from middle-aged skeptics who
claimed to have tested their naïve trust in the words of Jesus when they
were young and found them empty. No matter how long and hard they
prayed, Santa did not bring the pony, Daddy did not get sober, Mommy did
not recover, and their older brother did not dodge that bullet in Vietnam.
These recovering believers do not carry guilt at having too little faith; they
have relieved themselves of the burden of being deceived by faith.

Perhaps some of us here today fit into one or the other of these re-
sponses to Jesus' words, taking them as true and therefore diminishing ourselves or regarding them as false in order to assert our own view of reality.
More likely, many of us probably vacillate between the two positions. We
don't know whether to blame ourselves for our failure in faith or to blame
Jesus for making a false equation between cause and effect.

I think that a closer examination of Luke's version of Jesus' statement—
the version that did not become normative in the tradition—may enable us
to think in a slightly different way about what Jesus may have been getting
at . . . or, since what Jesus actually meant by what he said is always difficult
to determine, at least what the Gospel of Luke has to teach us.

We notice first that in Luke the statement about faith does not mention prayer and does not speak of a mountain. Jesus' declaration is no less
paradoxical—telling a mulberry bush to transplant itself to the sea and having it happen—but it is humbler, smaller, even more domestic. A mulberry
bush is considerably smaller than a mountain.

Then we notice that the statement in Luke does not serve as instruction on how the disciples are to perform wonders as spectacular as those
Jesus works, withering a fig tree or healing an epileptic child. Instead, Luke
places Jesus' statement about faith between two other statements. The first
concerns the need to forgive an erring brother or sister who causes a little
one to sin. Jesus concludes this saying with these words: "And if he wrongs
you seven times in one day and returns seven times and says, 'I am sorry,'
you should forgive him." It is at this precise point that the disciples ask Jesus
to "increase our faith."

We note further that Jesus does not stop talking after speaking of the mulberry bush and the sea. He continues speaking with another extended saying—it is in our Gospel reading this morning—about a master and a servant. In short, Luke does not connect the need for a larger faith to the working of great deeds, but to the basic living out of our lives.

The greater faith needed to forgive the constantly offending brother or sister is obvious. We all recognize the grinding effect of life with others and the way it saps our spiritual resources. But what are we to make of Jesus' saying about masters and servants?

The saying challenges us because it asks us to adopt two different perspectives, or, rather, asks us to shift perspectives without warning. Jesus starts off by appealing to his listeners as though they were people who owned slaves, and he elaborates onthe expectations of slave owners: they would not have their slaves eat immediately when they came in, even if they had spent the day plowing a field or shearing the sheep. Instead, masters would expect slaves to wait on the master in the household, cooking and waiting on table. Only then could the slave eat and drink and take rest. Jesus agrees with the imagined slave owners that they would have no particular gratitude for the slave's work; they were not doing the master a favor, but were doing what the master commanded.

But at this point, Jesus asks his listeners to adopt the perspective of the slaves rather than that of the masters: "So should it be with you," he says, "when you have done all that you have been commanded, say, 'we are unprofitable slaves; we have done what we were obliged to do.'"

In our age, this passage is extraordinarily difficult to hear. We don't want to think of ourselves as masters, and we sure don't want to be slaves. But if we use our imagination a little, we can push past the surface differences in our social words and appreciate the basic point. But what is the point?

I think the point of this entire sequence of sayings is that human life is difficult. Much of what we do is in service to others, doing what we are obliged to do rather than what we want to do. And much of our labor is thankless. Likewise, much of our life together is a matter of forgiving and forgiving over again hurts that are done to us. None of this is easy.

This is not, I submit, a bitter or cynical assessment. It is simple truth. When all is said and done, the life of faith is one of being unprofitable slaves who do what they are obliged to do.

A larger faith, a big-enough faith, is not demanded by the desire to throw either mountains or mulberry bushes into the sea. It is, rather, the slow slog through our all-too-ordinary, repetitious, anxious, and less-than-special days that needs a larger faith.

Faith, and the prayer of faith, is not a matter of making things happen, a technique for changing reality. Faith and the prayer of faith are rather the conditions of suffering existence itself, the humble, predictable, and patently painful living our life through the long decline to what seems the ultimate closure, and which, only because of that faith, can be perceived as our opening to God.

The larger faith that we need from Jesus is not one that seeks to remove troubles but the one that enables us to creatively embrace the troubles that are the very stuff of our existence. It takes a larger faith to forgive a brother or sister who hurts us seven times a day every day. It takes a larger faith to do what is asked of us every day without enough rest and with little thanks.

How do we know this? Not simply from what Jesus tells us, but from what Luke's Gospel shows us Jesus to be. Jesus is the one who, at the moment of his death by execution, says of those killing him, "Father, forgive them, for they do not know what they are doing" (Luke 23:34). And Jesus is the one who, before dying as a slave for the sake of his brothers and sisters, shares bread and wine as his sacrificial body and blood and says to them at the meal, "Let the greatest among you be as the youngest, and the leader as the servant. For who is greater, the one who is seated at table or the one who serves? Is it not the one seated at table? I am among you as the one who serves" (Luke 22:26–27).

PRAYER WITH PERIPHERAL VISION[1]

Luke 18:9–14

My sisters and brothers in Christ, even if Jesus were not known for anything else, he would be remembered and revered as one of humanity's greatest storytellers.

Jesus did not spin lengthy yarns. He crafted wonderful parables that, in astonishingly few words, captured an entire world and penetrated to the heart of human existence. It is one of the unexpected but lovely aspects of the incarnation that the human Jesus through whom God chose to reveal himself most fully was also an artist. The parables of Jesus remind us that truth and beauty alike reveal God.

The parables recounted by the evangelist Luke are especially memorable for being both beautiful and true. It is Luke alone who has Jesus tell such striking stories as the good Samaritan, the lost coin, the prodigal son, the unjust steward, Lazarus and Dives. He weaves these powerful short stories into his larger narrative and has concentrated them in his account of Jesus' long journey to Jerusalem.

This lengthy journey narrative extends from chapters 9 to 19 of his Gospel and is almost entirely Luke's own literary creation. Jesus certainly traveled to Jerusalem to meet his death at the hand of his enemies. But the journey is simply mentioned by Matthew and Mark. In contrast, Luke uses this journey as a frame within which he includes some of his most distinctive sayings from Jesus.

In this journey narrative, Jesus the prophet moves inexorably toward his suffering and death in Jerusalem. As he moves steadily toward his destiny, Jesus is constantly teaching. To those who oppose the prophet's call to repentance because they see no need to repent, he issues words of warning and rejection. To the crowds surrounding him, he speaks words of warning

1. The Chi Rho Institute, Eugene, Oregon, October 24, 2004.

and also of invitation. To those from the crowd who have already become his disciples, his students, Jesus speaks words of instruction. He teaches his followers about the proper use of possessions, and power, and prayer. These words of Jesus continue to resonate among those who even now hear his call and seek to learn from him as his students—people like you and me, who have gathered here in his name this morning.

Before listening more closely to the parable we have heard this morning, the parable about prayer involving a pharisee and a tax collector, it is helpful to remember two further aspects of Luke's Gospel.

The first is that, throughout Jesus' journey to Jerusalem, his disciples are drawn from those considered to be sinners by the religious elite of the day, especially the Pharisees. The sinners included tax collectors, men who got rich skimming from the taxes they collected from the poor for the rulers. In that same journey, Luke makes clear that the primary opponents of the kingdom proclaimed by Jesus are the Pharisees, the religious elite in Judaism (15:1–2).

The second is that, throughout Luke's Gospel, prayer is more than an optional act of piety. It is the essential element in a life of faith. The topic of prayer is never trivial. And on this long journey, Jesus has shared with his followers the prayer he himself says to the Father and has instructed them on the need to persevere in prayer.

Indeed, immediately before the parable we have heard this morning, Jesus speaks another parable to his followers specifically on this topic of perseverance in prayer (18:1–8). It is the remarkable story of the widow who so pesters the unjust magistrate that he finally gives in to her demands. We note that Jesus' closing question does not concern prayer but faith: "When the Son of Man comes, will He find faith on earth?"

For Luke, prayer is faith's essential expression. If we have faith, we pray. If we do not pray, we have no faith. Prayer reveals who we are before God. And how we pray shows the character of our relationship with God. It is no accident that Luke, more than the other evangelists, shows us Jesus praying at all the critical moments of his ministry: his baptism, his agony in the garden, his death on the cross. In Luke's account, the transfiguration of Jesus in the presence of his closest disciples happens while he is praying. The message is clear: the true identity of a person is revealed in prayer.

As we approach this parable, then, we need to keep those two points in mind. First, because Jesus does not tell the parable to his disciples as a positive instruction on prayer, but directs it instead to his showily pious opponents, those who "trusted in their own righteousness and despised everyone else." And second, because the way these two men pray tells us everything about their way of being in the world.

So how should we listen to the parable? We will not listen well if we hear it only as a tale told to people long ago rather than as a story told also to us. And we will not listen well if we think of it only as a lesson about styles of prayer and not about our entire existence before God.

We will listen well, I think, only if we acknowledge that, in some fashion or another, all of us here are among those who "trust in their own righteousness and despise all others," only therefore if we identify with the Pharisee rather than the tax collector, and therefore hear the parable not as a word of comfort about how well we are doing but as a word of challenge about how much we need to learn and how much we need to be changed.

If we transposed the two characters in the story into our own world, those of us here gathered would instinctively identify much more with the Pharisee than the tax collector. Pharisees were Jews who were most intently devoted to the traditions of Israel. They formed study groups and pledged to each other to be as faithful to all God's commands as possible. They ate fellowship meals to strengthen their bonds of unity. They resisted the corrupting influences of foreign ways. They tried to be as righteous as possible precisely in the way Moses had prescribed. They were like we are, good and pious Americans who pay our taxes and try to live decent lives.

In contrast, the tax collectors were Jews who were willing to betray the traditions of their people. They worked for the foreign occupiers—the Romans—who exploited and impoverished the Jewish population with their excessive taxes. They were willing to cooperate with such foreign oppressors in order to secure their own livelihood and became rich by cheating even the bosses. In today's terms, they could be seen as street-level drug dealers or even the small-time loan sharks associated with organized and international crime.

The shock of reversal in Jesus' parable depends on us getting these identifications right. We should regard the Pharisee as just like us, and the tax collector just like those you and I consider a threat to us and our values.

Nothing in Jesus' description of the Pharisee suggests that he was not a righteous man according to the measure of the law. He fasted twice a week. He gave tithes on his whole income. And he was a moral person: he was not avaricious, he was not dishonest, he was not sexually immoral. Or, to put it positively: he shared his possessions, he spoke the truth, and he was

122

faithful to his wife. Who can complain about such virtues? Are they not the very ones we would like to embody? Don't we, in fact, internally resent and externally complain about people who lie, and cheat, and take advantage of others?

So what is the problem in his prayer? Why does Jesus declare at the end that it was the tax collector who went home justified—that is, in right relationship with God—while the pious Pharisee did not? The statements at the beginning and at the end of the story give us clues. Luke tells us at the start that Jesus spoke this parable to those who trusted in their own righteousness and despised everyone else. And at the end, he repeats a statement that he had made earlier concerning people who sought the best places at a banquet: "Those who exalt themselves will be humbled, while those who humble themselves will be exalted." Humbled by whom, and exalted by whom? By God.

In light of this framing, let's look more closely at the prayer spoken by each man, remembering that for Luke, the way we pray reveals also the truth about ourselves. Note first the posture of prayer. The Pharisee "takes up a position" in the temple area, whereas the tax collector "stands at a distance and does not lift his eyes to heaven." In the first case, the posture of "taking a position" denotes a consciousness of belonging. In the second case, the body language of distance and lowered gaze belongs to one who knows he does not belong and is unsure of a positive reception. And quite right! The Pharisee does belong as a certified member of the pious. The tax collector is an interloper, a notorious outsider.

We note next the words of each in prayer. They both begin "O God" but then move in different directions. The tax collector prays to God and asks that God show mercy toward him. And he needs it. He is a sinner. It is appropriate that he humble himself. But now look at the Pharisee. Jesus says that he "spoke this prayer to himself." His prayer is directed not to God but to himself. And his words are all about himself.

He thanks God because he is not like all others—they are all sinners, we are to understand, while he is not. And then he makes the comparison personal. He thanks God that he is not like "this tax collector." Here is truly prayer with peripheral vision. The Pharisee's prayer reveals him to be one who trusts in his own righteousness and despises others. He comes before God as the winner in a morality competition. He asks God to consider his virtue in contrast to this fellow standing next to him in the temple. He needs nothing from God and therefore can receive nothing from God. He is the one who exalts himself and therefore, in God's eyes, has nowhere to go but down.

It is easy to take this as caricature. Surely Jesus exaggerates in his portrayal and in his warning. And perhaps you do not need this warning. But I do.

When I was a young man, I was a Benedictine monk, and I came to understand very well how I could be righteous without much reference to God at all. Not only was I living under a rule and an abbot a way of life that was demonstrably nobler and more difficult than that lived by those who were not monks (or so I then thought), but even within the monastery, the temple area, I was capable of taking a position and praying to myself: "Thank God I attend the divine office every hour; thank God I keep the pitch when chanting the psalms, not like these lazy brothers who go off tune; thank God I keep silence when the rule says to and do not whisper like those others over there; thank God that I fast more than the other monks, that I wear the shabbiest clothes, that I perform the most severe penances. Thank you, God, that I am me."

And even when I had left the monastery, and even after I had sinned most publicly and frequently while in my all-too-ordinary condition, I still managed, whenever I eked out a spurt of hard work, or a moment of piety, or a smidgeon of goodness, or a scrap of generosity, to turn it at once into something that I could claim as a possession, and more than a possession, as a basis for comparison to others. "Look at me," I say to myself, "how hard I work, how pious I seem, how good I am to others, how generous." Even when my life declares me to be a tax collector and a sinner, I am able to deceive myself and pray only to myself about myself.

But maybe that is just me.

ACTING ON FAITH[1]

Luke 17:11–19

My brothers and sisters in Christ, I am far more anxious standing before you this morning than I was Friday evening for my formal lecture. Preaching is a more serious business than teaching. As a teacher, I can stand outside my subject as an expert. But the preacher stands under the judgment of the word. Teaching can afford to be abstract because it mainly feeds the mind. Preaching must be specific because it directs our hearts. Preaching can't simply talk about Scripture as though it were a historical artifact, the way a teacher can even in Sunday School. The preacher needs to bring Scripture to bear on our lives this Sunday morning in Fort Wayne on October 14, 2007.

If I were your pastor and preached to you every week, I would still be anxious, but I would have more confidence in the practical pertinence of my words. I would share your everyday life, listen to your stories, and know of your week's good and bad news. As one among you, I could at least be sure that I was listening to this reading from the Gospel of Luke with ears like yours and know how this text touches us in very specific ways.

But as a guest preacher, I cannot be sure that what I say is in any fashion useful to you. So, like all guest preachers, I must attend even more closely to the text of Scripture in the hope that it can, as it so frequently does, speak truth to us whoever we are and in whatever conditions we live.

In today's reading, such close attention is particularly required. This apparently straightforward and artless story of Jesus healing ten lepers, one of them a Samaritan, turns out to be anything but straightforward and artless. It challenges our usual assumption that we can simply listen and then act. It demands of us some thinking. In such cases, it is best to move from

1. Plymouth Congregational Church, Fort Wayne, Indiana, October 14, 2007.

that we do know (or at least think we know) to what we know we don't understand.

Here are some things we know.

From a literary analysis, we know that Luke's Gospel distinctively portrays Jesus as God's prophet who announces God's vision for the world and challenges the world's accepted norms: he announces good news to the poor, and in his actions, he reaches out to all those the world demeans as poor: the sick, the demon-ridden, those put on the margins of society because they are women, or children, or regarded as sinners. Jesus opens his arms to them all, for God's kingdom is made up of such as them.

We also know that the section of Luke's Gospel where our story occurs is one that Luke has carefully composed: it is the long journey of Jesus, the prophet from Galilee, to the city of Jerusalem, where he will face death at the hands of those who reject God's vision for the world that the prophet Jesus announces and enacts. As Jesus moves toward his destiny in Jerusalem, Luke portrays him as constantly speaking: the crowds he calls to repentance; those joining his movement he teaches about prayer, possessions, and perseverance; and to his enemies he speaks parables of rejection.

Among all these sayings, Luke interposes only five healings: of a person possessed (11:14), of a crippled woman (13:10–17), of a man with edema (14:1–6), of these ten lepers (17:11–19), and of a blind beggar (18:35–43). The placement of each healing makes clear that Luke uses these stories the way he uses parables, to instruct his readers about the kingdom that Jesus proclaims.

Getting even closer to our passage, we know also that Luke places this healing of ten lepers between a speech of Jesus in response to his apostles who ask him to increase their faith (17:5) and a hostile question from the Pharisees concerning when the kingdom of God would arrive (17:20). To the request of the apostles, Jesus responds with a statement on the power of faith and the dispositions of slaves. To the Pharisees, Jesus declares that "the kingdom of God does not come through close scrutiny, with someone saying, 'look, here it is,' or 'look, there it is.' Look, the kingdom of God is among you." Luke's placement of this story, in short, gives us permission to interpret the healing of the lepers in light of the kingdom that is forming around Jesus on the basis of faith. So, we know all this pretty confidently from looking at Luke's literary arrangement.

We can also state some things fairly confidently about the characters in this story from the study of history. We recognize Jesus as the one who crosses boundaries erected by humans to separate from each other: he touches the sick and the dead, he eats with sinners.

We know also that there was a real and deep hostility between Jews and Samaritans, the kind of hostility that exists between next-door neighbors who share a history but have been fighting for generations about whose version of that history is correct. We caught a glimpse of that hostility, in fact, at the very start of Jesus' journey, when Samaritan villages refused to accept the scouts of this Jewish prophet, and Jesus had to restrain his Jewish disciples from calling down fire from heaven on them (9:51–54). Yet—such is the surprising character of Luke's Jesus!—we also have heard Jesus making a Samaritan, not the priest or the Levite, the hero of his story illustrating love of neighbor (10:29–37).

We also know a considerable amount about the social implications of leprosy in ancient Israel. I say social implications, because the actual physical condition remains obscure. The term "leprosy" could be applied to a variety of scabs or scales or markings, not only on the human body, but also on buildings and utensils. Because the syndrome was not understood, it was feared. And because it was feared, it was quarantined. The person designated as a leper—and it was a social designation—was removed from the common life of the people, including the life of worship. The fear of contamination condemned men and women to live apart from their friends and families and outside any inhabited place. The book of Leviticus commands: "The one who bears the sore of leprosy shall keep his garments rent and his head bare, and shall muffle his beard. He shall cry out, 'Unclean, Unclean.' As long as the sore is on him, he shall declare himself unclean, since he is in fact unclean. He shall dwell apart, making his abode outside the camp" (Lev 13:45–46).

Leprosy is the classic instance of social stigma. We are not surprised, then, to find bands of lepers outside the walls of cities, begging from those passing by. They are in bands, because those stigmatized can survive only among fellow exiles. They are begging, because they have been removed from any gainful employment and must depend utterly on those who still have work. In short, lepers are outcast and poor in every meaningful sense of the terms. Think of homeless men with AIDS under the highway overpasses where no one else will go. Human beings no longer fully human, both frightened and frightening.

Finally, we also know about priests within Israel. Their job was maintaining the purity of the worshiping people. They had to declare unclean those who in their judgment were marked with the disfigured skin associated with leprosy. They also had to judge whether those presenting themselves as without sores were in fact cleansed of this dread condition. Such judgments naturally meant that the leper, male or female, had to get naked and be examined from head to toe. Even when declared free from his or her former blemish, the leper still had to undergo an extensive series of ordeals in order to win full acceptance within the community of the pure (Lev 14:1–32). The priests did not make anyone clean but were the gatekeepers of social and ritual acceptance.

Knowing all this, we still find much in the story that is puzzling. What are we to make of Jesus traveling "through Samaria and Galilee," which is geographically impossible? Why does Luke use four distinct terms for what happened to the lepers: mercy, cleansing, healing, and being saved? Why does the Samaritan not obey Jesus' clear command to show himself to the priest? Why does Jesus praise him, but at the same time designate him as "this foreigner?" What does Luke mean by his "being saved by faith," and how did the Samaritan's actions show faith? And what are we to understand about the kingdom of God from this strange account?

Perhaps Luke's vague geographical notice is intentional. It suggests that Jesus is in an ambiguous territory between clear boundaries. In places where it is difficult to distinguish nationalities—think of the Balkans—it is more necessary to maintain other kinds of distinctions, such as that between clean and unclean. The Samaritan, in this case, is doubly stigmatized. He is both a leper and a foreigner in a place of unclear boundaries. He bands together with other lepers out of necessity, but even within that group, his foreignness marks him as different. But he too needs to eat, and he joins this temporary band of the stigmatized as they approach the Jewish prophet and ask him for money. The cry "teacher, have mercy" can just as well, and perhaps more accurately, be translated "teacher, give us alms." We can recognize here the cry of the homeless in our streets: "Do you have a quarter?"

When Jesus tells them all to go show themselves to the Jewish priests, he starts off with his temporary companions. Only we—and we assume, Jesus—know that this hated Samaritan is not going to be recognized as clean by Jewish priests. He is a Samaritan, unclean, as the Talmud says, from birth (as a Samaritan).

Now as the band heads toward the priests, they all discover themselves cleansed of their sores. The encounter with Jesus—his response to their cry for help—healed them from their leprosy. Nine of the (we assume Jewish) lepers continue on to the priests who can certify their readmittance to the cultic people. It's the way it's done. They are only singly stigmatized. Their own society can again embrace them.

Only the Samaritan perceived that he had been healed (the Greek word also means "being saved"). Healing is something more than cleansing. Being clean means being acceptable to the community; healing means being restored to one's full humanity. And this is a gift that can only be given by God. It was this acceptance by God that the Samaritan perceived. He therefore turned back from the futile and superficial social acceptance test administered by the Jewish priests and the ordeal that would, in any case, leave him outside the people so long as he remained a foreigner.

So, the Samaritan turns back toward Jesus, glorifying God with a loud voice. He publicly proclaims the gift of God's acceptance through his shouts of praise. More than that, he comes to Jesus and falls at his feet, giving him thanks. Here is where we see the Samaritan's faith. He acts on the fact of his healing and expresses his faith physically. He approaches the prophet—which he could not formerly do as one stigmatized by leprosy—and falls at his feet. He acts as one who is, in fact, clean, as one who is healed. He crosses boundaries because the boundaries were not created by God but by humans, and God's prophet has cleansed and healed him in a way that no human could.

It is the Samaritan's trust in his healing, and his acting on that trust, that reveals his faith and saves him, that is, draws him into the new community being formed around the prophet Jesus—the kingdom of God forming "among them." This community is not to be constituted by rules concerning clean and unclean but by the gift of God that liberates humans from such artificial marks of stigma and restores them together to a shared humanity.

The story of the Samaritan leper fits well within Luke's context. It provides an answer to the disciples' request that they be given an increase of faith: it tells us that faith increases by being acted upon. And it responds to the Pharisees' query about the coming of the kingdom of God: it is being formed around the prophet Jesus whenever humans are healed of the stigmata that divide them and then come together as those equally blessed by God.

The story invites us this morning to identify both with Jesus, who saves through faith, and with the Samaritan, who was saved through faith.

Like the Samaritan, each one of us has found his or her way here to give glory to God and thanksgiving to Jesus because of our faith in the ways God's gracious rule has found us and healed us, despite all the ways in which we have mutually excluded and stigmatized each other.

And because we have been gifted with the same prophetic Spirit that was his, we can also, like Jesus, act out the good news of God's kingdom by reaching out in faith across all those boundaries erected by fear in our own world, by refusing to call unclean those whom God has created clean, with faith welcoming into our presence even those whom, because they are different, we are tempted to fear and to flee.

DISCERNING GOD'S WILL[1]

Acts of the Apostles 15:1–21

M y sisters and brothers in Christ, the Acts of the Apostles tells us of the most important decision ever made in the history of the church. It was a decision made within some twenty years of Jesus' death and resurrection. An assembly of apostles and elders and ordinary believers in Jerusalem—all of them raised as Jews and all of them loyal to Judaism—decided to accept gentiles into their movement without requiring of them that they become Jewish, without their having to be circumcised and observing the law of Moses.

The ones making the decision probably had no sense of its far-ranging consequences, but, in effect, they opened the way to Christianity becoming a world religion rather than another Jewish sect, and they opened the way for you and me to be followers of a Jewish Messiah on the basis of faith rather than on the basis of our birth.

The meeting really happened. It is reported independently by the apostle Paul in his Letter to the Galatians (2:1–10). Although the details of Paul's report differ considerably from those in the Acts account, such differences actually confirm the basic historicity of the event: Jewish-Christian leaders met in Jerusalem and decided on the legitimacy and freedom of the Gentile mission.

Luke's version in Acts is later than Paul's, and is undoubtedly idealized, but his way of telling the story provides us this morning with the opportunity to appreciate both the surprising nature of the decision itself and the subtle process of discernment that led to the decision.

The decision to accept gentiles without qualification should still shock and surprise us, even though, as gentile Christians, you and I might be tempted to think, "Of course God wanted us to be included in his people;

1. First Presbyterian Church, Atlanta, Georgia, March 2013.

isn't it all about us?" In fact, there was nothing about the decision that was obvious and much that was risky.

The whole point of being a Jew, after all, was not to be a gentile. Israel was to be a people set apart by its relationship with the one God. It was not to be like the nations, who were unclean by nature and often filthy in practice. The gentiles were regarded as promiscuous both in their worship and in their sexual practices. How to stand apart from the gentiles as God's unique people was spelled out by the law of Moses, especially in commandments concerning worship and diet. A really serious Jew would avoid coming into contact with gentiles and would certainly never eat with gentiles, since in the ancient world table fellowship was regarded as more intimate than even sex. Jews ate with other Jews. The problem with gentiles is that they would eat with anyone.

Given all this, how could believers in a Jewish Messiah share table fellowship with those who were defined by Jewish law as unclean?

The entire witness of Scripture supported the negative view of gentiles in their unclean condition. To be sure, the prophets expressed the hope that gentiles would be converted to the one God of Israel and be joined to the people (e.g., Isa 42:1–6). But such admission of those called proselytes must always involve their accepting and practicing the customs of Israel, such as circumcision, and require of them observing the commandments of the law of Moses.

In the debate that started in Antioch and that led to the council in Jerusalem, therefore, the position held by the Pharisaic party of believers was, by the measure of Scripture alone, absolutely correct. If gentiles were to gain admission to God's people, it could only be through becoming Jews.

How, then, could these first believers—all of them Jews, remember—meet together and decide against the clear and consistent testimony of Scripture and all their previous understanding? They could do so because they paid attention to the way God was at work among them. They decided on the basis of what they learned, not from ancient texts, but from the Spirit of the living God in the lives of contemporary people.

Just as remarkable as the decision made by our forebears is the manner in which they reached that decision. To grasp this, we need to remember the backstory to this council that Luke has provided in earlier chapters of Acts, above all in the progression of events and experiences beginning in Acts 10 and extending to the passage we have read this morning. Luke shows us that the church's surprising decision was prepared for by a long process of discernment.

It started privately and quietly. A gentile soldier—someone doubly due the contempt of loyal Jews—is described as a righteous man who engages in prayer and good deeds. When he is at prayer, he experiences a puzzling command to summon a certain Simon Peter. At the very same moment, this Peter was also experiencing a vision in prayer that was even more puzzling: God seemed to be commanding him to eat all sorts of food displayed before him, without discriminating between clean and unclean (Acts 10:1–16).

As Peter puzzled over the meaning of this vision, the messengers from the gentile soldier Cornelius arrived and told Peter of the centurion's vision. The Holy Spirit then prompted Peter to go with these gentiles "without discrimination" or "without hesitation." And he did. Although, as he told Cornelius's household when he arrived, it was not lawful for him to mingle with gentiles, he nevertheless entered the pagan's house and listened as Cornelius repeated to him a personal account of his religious experience. Peter then stated, "I have come to realize that God does not have favorites, and that anybody, of any nationality, who fears God and does what is right, is acceptable to God" (10:17–35).

This most stunning insight—whose implications we have not yet fully appreciated—came to Peter not from his reading Scripture, but from his paying close attention to his own experience and the experience of the outsider, Cornelius. He learned the meaning of his own obscure vision through the narration of Cornelius's experience.

So, Peter proclaims the good news about Jesus to this Cornelius's gentile household, and as he does so, the Holy Spirit falls on his listeners. Peter and the other Jewish believers who had come with him conclude that because these Gentiles had received the same Spirit that they had in the beginning, they should be baptized. And they were (10:36–48).

What a dazzlingly swift progress this was, inspired by the Holy Spirit and responded to by humans willing to listen to the implications of their own experience and that of others, even when they were not at all sure where such faithful obedience would lead.

But there is more to Luke's story. Discernment leading to hard decisions rarely follows an entirely smooth path. Peter and his Jewish companions are summoned before the elders in Jerusalem to give an account not of their having baptized pagans but of their having gone in and eaten with pagans. Note the deep-seated character of the leaders' resistance. God may have accepted these gentiles by giving them the Holy Spirit, but it is another thing entirely to eat with them. Remember how intimate the fellowship of the table was considered in antiquity.

Peter simply and straightforwardly relates the entire story over again, from Cornelius's vision to the baptism of Cornelius's whole household. Peter states that refusing gentiles baptism when they already had been given the same Spirit as Jewish believers would amount to resisting God. The elders agree that God had given "repentance to life" to the gentiles. But the issue of eating together, of overcoming cultural-religious barriers, still remains to be decided (11:1–18).

And now, to show us how the inclusion of the gentiles was truly God's desire and not the private decision of Peter or simply the local decision of the Jerusalem elders, Luke's narrative expands: he tells us how certain anonymous preachers began to preach to gentiles directly and converting them to the Lord (11:19–21). This initiative is carried further by Paul and Barnabas. When the Holy Spirit directed the church in Antioch to send them out on mission (13:1–3), and when they were stymied by the resistance of their Jewish listeners, they also turned explicitly to the conversion of the gentiles (Acts 13:46–48; 14:1, 27).

By this means, Luke intends us to understand that the Holy Spirit, working through recognized leaders as well as through anonymous preachers, was bringing about something new, something that grew so large that it became necessary for the church in a formal fashion to declare for or against what the Spirit seemed to be showing it in the experience of so many people.

The need for the church as a whole finally to discern and decide, Luke shows us, is caused by controversy. When God does something so new, it is not going to be obvious to everyone that the new is actually from God. Disagreement and dissent are legitimate elements of discernment. Thus, Luke portrays a vigorous controversy in the church at Antioch that leads to the sending of a delegation to Jerusalem to settle the matter (15:1–2). In Jerusalem, the controversy continued, as one party insisted, on the basis of the testimony of Scripture, that gentiles needed to become Jews to be accepted fully into the people of God, and others insisted, on the basis of the testimony of the experience of themselves and others, that gentiles should be received into full communion with no requirement of changing their ethnic identity.

We know how the conflict was resolved because we sit and stand here today as gentile Christians. But four aspects of the decision reported by Acts are especially important for us as we consider discernment in our own time.

The first is that while allowing gentiles in without requiring circumcision or observance of the law, the council crafted a compromise position, demanding of gentile believers certain basic commitments that would enable Jewish believers to have table fellowship with them without being deprived of their own ethnic customs (15:20–21, 29). When the church no longer had a significant Jewish population, the so-called apostolic decree was no longer needed. But the lesson is that even radical decisions can require compromise for the sake of unity.

The second aspect is that the church truly did decide on the basis of personal witness to the experience of God. Not only Paul and Barnabas, but also Peter and James concurred in accepting the inclusion of the gentiles because of the activity of the Holy Spirit revealed in the stories of many and diverse persons (15:2–4, 7–11). "How can we," they said, "test God?" To say this means that one must truly believe that God is at work in human lives.

The third aspect is that although the church decided on the basis of experience rather than on the basis of Scripture alone, it by no means abandoned its devotion to Scripture. But it interpreted Scripture in a new way because of what God had shown them in their own lives. James declares not that the things happening agree with the Scripture, but that Scripture agrees with these things that are happening (15:15–18). The difference is slight but important.

The fourth aspect is that the story beginning with two separate and individual experiences of God leads at last to the church's more adequate grasp of its own identity. When Peter saw the Holy Spirit fall on the gentiles in Cornelius's house, he concluded that they had received the same gift as Jewish believers had at the beginning. But now, in light of all the narratives he has heard, Peter declares a deeper understanding, showing at last the full meaning of his initial dream about clean and unclean food: he declares that "we are saved by faith in the gift that is the Lord Jesus Christ in the same manner as they are" (15:11). Peter sees that he is not part of the people because he is a Jew but because, like the gentiles, he has faith. God's acceptance of outsiders reveals to those who think of themselves as insiders the true basis of their own acceptance by God.

My brothers and sisters in Christ, we can rejoice that our forebears in the faith had the courage to discern the work of God's Holy Spirit in their lives and to make the decision that gave birth to us who are gentile Christians. But that discernment and decision also provides an example that challenges us in the church today, for the presence and the power of the living God continue to work among us, often in unexpected and shocking ways, and continue to call the church to the kind of attentive listening that is the essence of faith.

TO SHARE ALL OF LIFE[1]

Luke 20:45–21:6

My sisters and brothers in Christ, this reading from Luke's Gospel reports three sayings of Jesus that should cause us to examine ourselves concerning our use of possessions.

We are not surprised by the harshness of Jesus' first and last statements that are directed at avaricious religious leaders and ostentatious patrons, because we recognize just those sorts of people in our own society. Those ancient scribes who postured piously in public were not so different from contemporary preachers who also "swallow the houses of widows" by means of their grandiose and self-serving projects.

And those "noble stones and offerings" that Jesus says will be destroyed along with the temple were the ancient equivalent of the memorial plaques and dedicatory inscriptions we see today in churches and on college campuses and civic buildings. Financial patronage operates much the same now as it did then: it still has its privileges, still demands that generosity be put on public display.

But our attention this morning is especially, and rightly, drawn to what Jesus had to say about the widow who put her small coins into the temple treasury. This treasury, we know, was the ancient Jewish poor box; the funds deposited in it were distributed to the needy. The woman who represented all the chronically needy in the ancient world gives what she has to others who are impoverished.

Jesus makes a double contrast, on one hand between the wealthy and the widow, and on the other hand between the gifts of the rich given out of their excess and the gift of the widow out of her destitution. Jesus says that the widow has given "more than all the rest," not because of the size of her gift, but because of its more radical character. By donating two of the

---

1. Stewardship Sunday at Oakhurst Baptist Church, Decatur, Georgia, 2014.

smallest coins then in circulation—think of our despised pennies—she was giving, Jesus says, all her *bios*, that is, everything that supported her own marginal existence. For Jesus, it appears, the measure of giving is less the amount than the cost.

Jesus' statement about the widow's giving her entire *bios*, or life, helps us to think about the ways we can use possessions faithfully, that is, precisely as an expression of our faith. What might giving our entire *bios* actually mean in the real-life circumstances of our lives now, as we seek to be faithful to God?

We can begin our thinking by reminding ourselves of the meaning of faith. We know that faith is not simply a matter of belief. We know that it is a matter of responding in trust and obedience to the living God. If faith were just a matter of belief, then we could cry "Jesus is Lord" or "God is One," put the appropriate sticker on the bumper of our car, drive off to the grocery, and never have to think about it again. But faith in the biblical sense, in the sense that we use it, only starts with belief. Authentic faith is a response of the whole person—mind, heart, body—to the living God, whose word summons us in every circumstance of our lives.

Because of this, faith is not something that can be expressed once for all. Faith must express itself every moment, moment by moment, of our lives. We cannot dispose of ourselves, or of our possessions, all in one grand gesture. As our life gets played out moment by moment, so must we dispose of ourselves (and our possessions) moment by moment, in response to the living God who presses on us at every moment—presses on us above all through God's continuing to bring the world into existence around and within us—so that every moment of our lives is a call from God that demands a response of trust and obedience. If our use of possessions is to be faithful, then, it cannot consist merely in a yearly pledge, or a single check, or even a grand donation. Like our faith itself, it must be through our response to every circumstance in which we find ourselves. Thus, it is very much a matter of our entire *bios*.

We also get closer to the implications of Jesus' words by remembering the wide range of things that we humans claim as possessions, and therefore can either grasp to ourselves or share with others. Possessions are not only those material things that we have been given or have earned or have purchased—our money, our homes, our cars, our toys—although those are the things we usually think of first. In fact, we claim ownership over many things that we consider as being under our power or control.

We can, for example, agree that we *are* bodies, but our language gives away that we also think—quite rightly in fact—that we also *have* what we call "our" bodies. We dispose of our bodies as the first of our possessions and as the most important symbol or expression of ourselves.

How we dispose of the body, where we put it, how we activate it, is essential to the response of faith in the living God. We can close off our bodies from the world, to others, to God. We can erect walls around our bodies in gated enclaves. Or, we can open our bodies to the world, to others, to God, with free access. Our material possessions, in turn, are in effect extensions of our bodies, so that in a very real sense, the way we dispose of the things we claim to own is also a form of *self-disposal*. If we say we are open to the world, yet cling tightly to all we have, we are deceiving ourselves.

But material things are only the most visible and obvious possessions. Look at all the other things over which we claim ownership! We "have" relationships: I "have" a wife—she will be surprised to learn. You "have" friends, associates, contacts. We "have" time, we "have" space, we "have" energy, we "have" ideas, we "have" visions, we "have" emotions. All of these are at our disposal. All of them we can either grasp or share. All of them can be expressions of faith in the living God. Even if we are in rags and live in a box under the interstate overpass, we have a body and therefore have time and space, and we can place them at the service of others.

The faithful use of possessions must, then, be an expression of our response of faith in the living God at every moment, and cannot, therefore, be taken care of all at once, but only moment by moment throughout our life. And our faithful use of possessions cannot only be of our money or other material things, but must include the disposition of our bodies and space and time and energy and ideas and emotions.

There is still one more thing we must consider if we seek to make our sharing of possessions an expression of faith in the living God. This last aspect is in some ways the most frightening and brings us close to the risky action of the widow.

It is this: our sharing of possessions must be determined not by what we want to give or think we should give, but by the need with which we are confronted in the others God places before us moment by moment through our lives. The measure is not what we want to give, but what they need to receive.

How we wish it were other! How we wish we could figure out our budget for the year, calculate our tithe, mail in the check, and be done with it. Or how comforting it would be if we could work out our weekly schedule to allow a certain time for sharing—of ideas, of energy, of space—so that when the time elapsed, we could return to our own projects.

But our desire for control is the exact opposite of obedient faith, which responds to the call of God in the specific and concrete circumstances of every moment of our lives.

God presents us at every moment what needs to be shared. This child needs changing, this child needs comforting, this one needs a time out. This stranger needs a meal, this one a bed, this one directions to shelter. This parent needs my financial help, this parent needs emotional support, this parent needs medical attention. My spouse at this moment needs my close attention and at another moment needs me to give her space. My community now needs my money, now my time, now my vision, now my patience.

Here is the reason why the obedience of faith is risky and costly and demands our very *bios*—the very stuff of our lives. It is moment by moment and never over. It includes all that we are and have. It is demanded according to the need of the other and not according to our plans for giving.

In sum, the obedience of faith and the faithful use of our possessions demand of us that we pay attention. What is it, we must ask, that is being asked of us in this time and space, and by these particular people God places with us this day? Without such attentiveness, faith is a posture rather than a practice. But with such attentiveness, our very lives are at risk. Such is the character of faith.

THE PROPHETIC CHURCH[1]

First Corinthians 12:12–26
Luke 4:14–30

My sisters and brothers in Christ, the Scripture passages we have just heard read invite us to think about the Holy Spirit. I don't mean that we should think doctrinally about the Holy Spirit as the third person of the triune life we call God, although that is not a bad way of thinking and one certainly appropriate in a church named for the Trinity!

I mean rather to think about the Holy Spirit in the way that Scripture itself does: as the unseen presence and power of God in creation, God's very breath that calls into being that which is not, God's very life enlivening dead bones, God's sovereign energy that summons prophets to bear witness within creation to God's will for creation.

I want to think with you this morning about the Holy Spirit as the Spirit of prophecy. But I do not want for us to think about this prophetic Spirit as something in the past about which Scripture speaks but about which we have no local knowledge. I hope rather that Scripture can provide us a lens through which we might perceive and appreciate the way God's prophetic Spirit continues to breathe among us today and to call us to witness.

How could there be a better topic for our thinking in this epiphany season, when the church celebrates the multiple ways God's Spirit has used the bodies created by God to reveal God's presence in the world?

Such thinking ought not to be too great a stretch for us. We have, after all, gathered here on this Sunday morning—the day of resurrection—precisely because we are convinced that just as Jesus was raised from the dead by God's power and was exalted to share fully in God's power and life, so as

1. Trinity United Methodist Church, Birmingham, Alabama, January 24, 2016.

to become, as Paul declares, "life-giving Spirit," so is the powerful Spirit of the resurrected Lord active among us when we gather this way in his name.

This conviction, supported by the evidence of God's transforming Spirit among us when we pray and act in Jesus' name, is what links us to the earliest believers, who out of such experiences and convictions wrote the narratives and letters we now call the New Testament.

Thus, when Luke's Gospel portrays Jesus in his hometown synagogue in Nazareth, it is as one already filled with the Holy Spirit and already working through the power of the Holy Spirit. When Jesus reads from the scroll of the prophet Isaiah concerning one who would be anointed with the Holy Spirit and proclaim good news to the poor and liberty to captives, and then announces in the presence of all that these very words of Scripture are fulfilled that day in him, ancient readers of this text, like us, recognized that the power at work in Jesus to call the outcast and drive out demons and heal the afflicted is precisely the same power that was at work among them.

And when Paul, in his First Letter to the Corinthians, speaks of the church as the body of Christ because all his readers in the church of Corinth had been baptized in the Holy Spirit and had been given to drink of that same Spirit, so that they were not simply a loose assemblage of like-minded and friendly people who happened to live in Corinth and needed somewhere to go Sunday morning, but were, in a very real sense, the bodily presence of the one who became life-giving Spirit, Paul asked his readers to understand, as we do now, that appearances can deceive, that ordinary suburban people can and do bear within them the presence and power of God's Holy Spirit, so that they, and we, are something more than a monument to organizational ambition, but are, in truth, God's means of manifesting God's presence in this suburb, this city, this small part of God's creation.

We have fellowship with the New Testament's first readers, then, because with them we acknowledge that the presence and power of God's Holy Spirit are not simply a reality of the past, but above all a reality in the present, specifically our present, here and now, in the city of Birmingham, Alabama. The power by which God raised Jesus from the dead to make him life-giving Spirit is the same power that speaks to us in these words of Scripture, that enlivens us through the sacraments, that transforms us into a body capable of manifesting God in our world.

But with our ancient sisters and brothers, we also are stirred by the same Spirit to ask how the prophetic Spirit of Jesus should be at work among and through us. We celebrate the gift that these texts disclose to us, yes, but are moved as well to ponder the mandate that they might impose on us in our day. To what prophetic task does God's prophetic Spirit summon us?

So let's look a bit more closely at how Luke in his Gospel actually portrays Jesus the Spirit-filled prophet. We see that the Spirit's work of liberating the captive and the afflicted does not take the form of establishing an academic center for messianic studies, or organizing resistance to Roman occupation of the land, or founding an ecologically sensitive alternative to a temple economy, or founding a community of the pure to compete with the Pharisees and Essenes. As Luke's subsequent narrative shows us, it consists in Jesus touching those whom he meets, one by one, and healing them. It consists of Jesus naming the evil powers that subjugate humans and driving them out. It consists of Jesus embracing the children who crowd around him. It consists of Jesus welcoming into his presence women and the outcast, of sitting at table with those ritually and morally suspect in the eyes of the pious.

The good news to the poor is precisely the way in which God, through the Spirit-guided body of Jesus, touches and accepts all those who in the eyes of the rich and powerful are beneath contempt. The messianic mission, it seems, is nothing more than Jesus putting his body in a position to touch and be touched by the bodies of others, without fear, without constraint, and without judgment. Jesus allowed the Spirit of God to be communicated in this simple fashion, body to body, individual to individual. Jesus appears in Luke's Gospel as the supremely free human person, who never seemed to have anything better to do than to be with those around him, and who considered that such intimate and direct physical contact was, in fact, liberating and joyous good news from and about God.

If the Corinthians, in turn, were to ask—and if we in Birmingham are to ask—how the prophetic spirit of Jesus ought to express itself in and through them—and us—Paul's response is remarkably consistent with Luke's portrayal. He does not suggest that the Corinthians should proclaim Jesus to everyone they meet. He does not demand that they reform the structures of the ancient household or city. He does not tell them to create a utopian society in which all differences of ethnicity and gender and status are eliminated. Instead, he tells them that they are called to be one body.

As the Corinthians—and we—individually were given sight when once they were blind, were freed of compulsions when once they were driven by evil powers, were healed of their physical and emotional scars, and were brought into a place of safety and sanity in a community shaped by the presence and power of God's Holy Spirit, so, Paul suggests, they are to be, simply, a source of light and vision to each other, a presence to each other that liberates from the captivities of anxiety and compulsion, a source of forgiveness one to another, fostering together amity and reconciliation where once there had been enmity and alienation.

The body of Christ, Paul tells the Corinthians—and us—is prophetic because it bears witness in and to the world of how God wants humans to live in fellowship. In this body, the Holy Spirit lives and moves in such fashion that each member is accepted and welcomed by every other member. This body is where the distinctive and irreplaceable role of each member is recognized and affirmed, where the weak do not threaten the strong but become the opportunity for the strong to share their strength, where those most in need are shown the most honor and support.

The mission of the church, these readings tell us, is not to produce more members or to provide more services or to alter society in our own image. It is rather to transform believers into disciples through practicing the ministry of simple bodily presence and care, and so to manifest within an angry and alienated world an embodied way of living that is Christ's own, enlivened by God's prophetic and Holy Spirit.

WORDS AT RITUAL MOMENTS

BAPTISM: THE VINE
AND THE BRANCHES[1]

First John 4:7–21
John 15:1–8

M y sisters and brothers in Christ, thank you for allowing me to share this weekend with you. I am especially pleased to join you as you welcome a new member into the body of Christ through the sacrament of baptism. Baptism, as you know, is always an Easter celebration. It is an initiation into the new life that we share because Jesus is, now and always, our resurrected Lord.

And this is very much the point I have been trying to make in my presentations to you this weekend.[2] The resurrection is not for us an event that happened long ago to someone else named Jesus, but is the most powerful reality that shapes our lives today, because Jesus as the exalted Lord is the life-giving Spirit who transforms our lives.

When we read Jesus in the Gospels from the perspective of this resurrection experience and conviction, we read him truly. And when we learn Jesus in this community through the sacraments—such as baptism—and the example of the saints, we learn him as he truly is.

Such learning of Jesus is profoundly in touch with the compositions of the New Testament. All of them were written from within communities of faith like this one. All of them perceive the human Jesus in light of believers' continuing experience of him as the One who enlightens and empowers them. Nowhere is this perspective more obvious than in the Gospel of John. When the evangelist composed this Gospel, the Paraclete promised

1. Saint Mary on the Highlands Episcopal Church, Birmingham, Alabama, May 3, 2015.

2. This was a typical two-lectures-and-a-sermon kind of weekend. My lectures were on learning Jesus in the context of the church.

by Jesus, namely the Holy Spirit, had already led the church into a further and deeper understanding of Jesus—what he had said and what he did and what he suffered. The Easter truth defined Christian faith in the first generation just as it does in ours.

Unlike the other evangelists, John does not report parables spoken by Jesus, those short stories about wheat and weeds, servants and kings, lost sheep and coins and sons that so tease our minds about the character of God's kingdom. Instead, John presents powerful and simple metaphors— images of water and light and bread—all of which point to the person of Jesus, understood by both John and his readers as the one who not only spoke to others in the past but also spoke to those in the present gathered in his name. "I am the light of the world," he has Jesus say, "I am the living bread come down from heaven."

Matthew and Luke have Jesus speak of a shepherd who left behind ninety-nine sheep so that he could search out the one sheep who was lost. John has Jesus describe the qualities of an authentic shepherd who calls each of his sheep by name, and whom the sheep follow because they know his voice (10:2–4), and then has Jesus declare of himself, "I am the good shepherd. I know my own and my own know me, as I know the Father and the Father knows me; and I lay down my life for the sheep" (10:14). This image of the shepherd communicates Jesus' relationship to the God whom he reveals, the intimate relationship between Jesus and those who are his own, and the gift of life that Jesus gives to them through his own death. As we read, so we understand: Jesus is our source of life, Jesus is our bond of intimacy, Jesus shows us the love of God.

It is no wonder that the image of Jesus as good shepherd was and is so pertinent to baptism, especially of infants: they are welcomed not only into a congregation of the faithful, but above all into the most intimately shared new life of God given through Jesus. They are known by name by the One who gives them this life, long before they are even aware of his name.

We heard read to us this morning the last of these remarkable metaphors that Jesus applies to himself in John's Gospel. It appears among his final words to his disciples before his death. He tells them, "I am the true vine, and my Father is the vinegrower" (15:1). The image echoes the prophet Isaiah's parable of the vineyard that was Israel planted by the Lord, from which he sought righteousness (Isa 5:1–7). As everywhere in the Fourth Gospel, though, the metaphor of the "true" vine, the "authentic" vine, the vine by which all other life must be measured, here recalls the intense intimacy of life existing between Jesus and his Father. The Father lives in him and he lives in the Father. And God has planted Jesus among humans so that he can be their source for this same shared life. So Jesus says, "I am the vine, you are the branches," and continues, "those who abide in me and I in them bear much fruit, for apart from me you can do nothing" (John 15:5).

Two important truths are implicit in the image of the vine and the branches, both truths profoundly pertinent to the sacrament of baptism. The first truth is that the branches are utterly dependent on the vine for their life. Thus we also in the church confess that we live by, are utterly dependent on, the life we receive as gift from Jesus our Lord, in the word of proclamation, in the grace of healing, in the sacraments, in the witness of the saints. We are not self-derived or self-sufficient. We are fed from the source, who is Jesus.

The second implied truth is that this shared source of life, this same sap that runs through each of our veins, draws us into a common identity. Because we drink the same Spirit, because we eat the same bread, because we drink the same wine that is drawn from the vine that is Jesus, we grow together as one body. Thus, the infant baptized here today is not merely listed in the parish registry of members, as though this were a country club. The newly baptized infant is instead drawn into a mutual and interdependent exchange of life that draws from the inexhaustible richness of the exalted Lord Jesus.

What a remarkable gift! What a cause of joy, to be—each of us, all of us—so immediately connected to the very source of life and to be—each of us, all of us—so closely joined together in such an intimate communion! As Jesus states, "I have said these things so that my joy may be in you, and that your joy may be complete" (15:11).

Jesus makes a third truth about the vine and branches explicit: the purpose of the vine is to bear fruit. Grapes cannot grow on a branch torn off the vine. So the fruit draws from the life of the vine itself. But the fruit, in turn, is to become food and drink for others, is to become a source of life for others. The fruit does not feed the vine. The fruit feeds the world. Jesus makes clear what the image of bearing fruit entails: "My Father is glorified in this, that you bear much fruit and become my disciples" (15:8). But what does becoming Jesus' disciples mean? "As the Father has loved me, so I have loved you; abide in my love" (15:9). And how do we abide in his love? By showing to each other—indeed, all others—the love he showed us: he says,

"This is my commandment, that you love one another as I have loved you" (15:12).

The dimensions of such love are spelled out magnificently in today's reading from the First Letter of John. God is love, and God's love for us has been shown to us through the sacrifice of his Son Jesus. It is not that we first loved God, but that God first loved us, and we learn what love truly means from the way God has loved us in Christ. And the way we honor God is simply by extending that love to those around us: "Beloved, since God loved us so much, we ought to love one another. No one has ever seen God. If we love one another, God lives in us, and His love is perfected in us" (1 John 4:11–12).

But if our love for each other is truly to be like God's love for us and follow the pattern that God showed us in Jesus, it must be more than a matter of affection or even good will and kind words. It must take the form of sometimes costly service and sacrifice. As John says earlier in this letter, "We know love by this, that He laid down His life for us—and we ought to lay down our lives for one another. How does God's love abide in anyone who has the world's goods and sees a brother or sister in need, and yet refuses to help? Little children, let us love not in word or speech, but in truth and action" (1 John 3:16–18).

This, in turn, brings us to a fourth and sobering truth about the vine and the branches. Those who do not bear the fruit that is life-giving love for others, Jesus tells us, will be branches that are cut off from the vine as useless. What? Yes. Jesus says, "He removes every branch from me that bears no fruit" (John 15:2). These branches have received life, but they do not share it. What good are they? Jesus says they are thrown away and wither: "Such branches are gathered, thrown into the fire, and burned" (15:6).

This is sobering, I suggest, but not really frightening, because we remember that bearing such fruit is not beyond our capacity. It is simply sharing the life and love that come to us in a constant stream from God. The goods of the world that we possess come to us as gifts from God; why should we not share them? The beauty and strength of our bodies are gifts of the Lord; why should we not use them for the good of others? The talents of our mind come to us from Another; shall we not give them to others? If our very life comes to us through the gift of life in Christ, shall we not also share that gift? The option, Jesus tells us, is to be thrown away as useless. And that seems fair enough.

There is, however, a final and much scarier truth embedded in Jesus' image. Jesus says, "Every branch that bears fruit he prunes to make it bear more fruit" (John 15:2). Then he adds, "You have already been pruned (or cleansed) by the word I have spoken to you" (John 15:3).

The same Greek word is translated as both "cleansed" and "pruned." But even someone with as little horticultural knowledge as mine knows that pruning involves the cutting away of branches, and sometimes very deep cutting indeed.

In the actual experience of the branch being cut, the distinction between getting pruned and getting hacked off and thrown away to be burned may appear too fine. Am I, in fact, being cut off from God? Or am I being pruned by God to bear more fruit? Is there an experiential difference? Does bearing fruit through sacrificial love look more like the desolation of despair than it does the ebullient joy of spiritual consolation? The witness of the mystics through the centuries suggests that this indeed might be the case.

There is much to think about here, but I want only to suggest that sharing with each other the love that God has shown each one of us in the death of Jesus—thus bearing fruit on the vine—is a serious business and not for the casual Christian. Just as John has warned us that love is more than a sentiment and fine words but requires a difficult physical and mental and emotional engagement with the needs of others, so these words of Jesus suggest that such love does not mean escape from or even relief of suffering and pain, but may elevate our levels of suffering and pain in a way we could never anticipate.

Baptism, we are reminded, means that we participate not only in the joy of Easter and the life of resurrection. Baptism plants us as well in the suffering and death of Jesus. Authentic Christian love always bears the scars of the One who gave his life that we too might live.

ORDINATION: EXEMPLARY LIFE[1]

Isaiah 6:1–8
Psalm 112:8–18
First Peter 5:1–4
Matthew 9:35–38

My brothers and sisters in Christ, ordaining people to the priesthood is a little tricky. It's not exactly like appointing policemen or firefighters. With them, we have clear job descriptions and expectations. We don't care what firefighters do in their spare time, so long as they get to the flames on time. What policemen do when not on the beat is no concern of ours, so long as they catch crooks when on the beat.

With priests, it's different. Priesthood does, to be sure, involve certain specific functions, like administering the sacraments, preaching, visiting the sick, and counseling—tasks that demand skills more complex than firefighting—but it also involves taking on a certain representative role within the Christian community. Christian ministry expresses Christian identity not only by doing certain things but by being a certain way. And there is where our troubles start.

From the beginning of the church down to the present, ministers have been ordained for service by the laying on of hands and prayer. We lay on hands to signify that this person is being set aside in a special way for God's work. We pray because we hope God has a better idea of what that means than we do.

Thus, this evening, the bishop and elders lay hands on Bill, and we pray together. And together we listen to the word of God as it comes to us in these snippets of texts from all over the Bible, hoping as we listen to gain a better idea of what we are doing: a slice of the prophet Isaiah, a few verses

1. At the ordination of William Shepherd to the Episcopal priesthood, Carmel, Indiana, May 25, 1983.

from Peter's First Letter, some lines from Psalm 132, and a piece of Matthew's Gospel. That we should sit still and pay attention to such fragments is fascinating in itself. Why don't we just pick out some long and impressive passage of the Bible that explains what Christian priests are and what they should do?

Wouldn't that make sense? Of course it would. But we can't do that, because there are no such passages. Christian ministry has developed enormously since the writing of Scripture. The New Testament, indeed, knew of no priests except those of the Mosaic variety and the great High Priest, Jesus. So there are not straightforward texts to explain what Bill should do or be and what we should expect of him.

What we have, instead, are bits and pieces, which we are obliged to put together in a coherent pattern as best we can. In this way, also, Christian ministry expresses Christian identity, for neither does any one of us have a comprehensive description of God's will for ourselves, even in the Bible. All of us must hear the word of God to us in fragments, just as we live our lives in fragments and not all at once. We are all required to put the stories we hear in Scripture and the stories we live every day in conversation, hoping that it will all come out coherently, but never having the luxury of being sure.

I don't mean to suggest that this is a bad thing. Just the opposite. I rejoice in the freedom God has given us in the gospel, and praise God that we are not constrained by law. But such freedom demands of us a responsible attentiveness both to the texts of Scripture and to our lives. If we fail to hear either, we may also miss the chance to better understand this ritual moment when Bill crosses over from one way of life to another, by our commission and with our support.

Although the texts we have heard read to us this evening have failed to give us a simple or single picture of Christian ministry, they do suggest to us three aspects of that ministry that we do well to ponder.

The scene from Isaiah in which the prophet encounters the holiness of God and is sent to proclaim God's word to the people reminds us of the *prophetic* character of the Christian priesthood. We ask of our priests not only the performance of ritual actions but the interpretation of our lives through God's word. We look for this first in the pulpit. We are bitterly disappointed—even when we do not admit it even to ourselves—when our preacher's words have become nothing but bromides and banal blessings. No, we ask the priest to go to the furnace of God's word and return to us with burning coals—words that at once reveal to us how unclean we are in the presence of God's holiness and that also cleanse our lips and hearts by the hearing of them.

We ask our priest also to speak in a prophetic voice about the specific shape of our lives in the world. We want to hear the *truth* spoken, not only about cosmic matters but also about the small affairs that preoccupy us in our daily lives. We ask the priest to be willing to live under God's word and to drag us as well under that saving judgment, even when—out of fear of healing—we do not wish it. We are all called to be a people formed by God's word, and we ask our priest to articulate that word for us.

The reading from the First Letter of Peter tells the elder, "Do not be domineering over those in your charge, but be examples to your flock" (1 Pet 5:3). The Christian minister is a leader of the community, not by force of law or even by force of personality, but because in the minister the community can find the pattern of the life it is called to live. The priest is to be an example.

But what sort of example? Do we ask of the priest the perfect display of all the virtues or unfailing consistency in spiritual sensitivity? No, for neither is that what it means to be Christian. The priest, rather, should be an example of what it means to measure one's life not by the norms of human success and not by the standards of the world but by the standards of God's kingdom. It is not meeting that measure that is important, but the willingness to stand under it. And this, no matter how inadequate one's performance.

We want the priest to be an example of the pattern of faith, which is a process of dying to self-interest through service to others. In this way, the priest is, in Peter's words, a "witness to Christ's sufferings." Such a pattern of life always involves suffering, for it always entails dying to the self through thousands of small cuts. We all seek to avoid such suffering. And that is precisely why we need a prophetic voice and a living example among us.

How does the priest fail to be such an example? When the priest no longer cares, when the priest holds the people to a standard the priest no longer lives under, when the priest serves for personal gain (in whatever coinage), when the priest forgets that all is gift and thinks only in terms of constraint.

The passage from Matthew's Gospel teaches us more about the measure of Christian ministry by showing it displayed perfectly in Jesus. We have heard in this passage that Jesus also was carrying out a ministry of preaching: he went about proclaiming the kingdom of God. He was also carrying out a ministry of healing. But the Gospel tells us more. It tells us that in the midst of all his activity, Jesus *saw* the crowds about him. And he *saw* their condition as one of harassment and helplessness. And he was filled with compassion. Each stage of his response deserves consideration.

First, he saw. A harder thing than we might think. When one is building programs—if not also buildings—and keeping schedules and being terribly busy being the visible and successful minister, it requires one to actually see and hear those around one as more than extensions of one's own energy and ambition.

But more than a simple personal awareness is required. It is necessary to perceive, beneath the veneer of bland ordinariness and casual good cheer that pervades church gatherings, the deep spiritual illnesses of the people. The priest must be able to diagnose spiritual malaise, recognizing it all the more accurately because knowing it also in the priest's own life.

To see the people, and to see that they are harassed and helpless, though, is still not enough. What matters most is to be moved by compassion, to care. This is, indeed, the most difficult aspect of the response of faith. For the priest, too, is human, and is preoccupied by the ambiguities and complexities of the priest's own harried existence, which also often feels helpless. The priest is most of the time just barely holding things together, like the rest of us. When we ourselves feel that we are just getting by, the stories and cries of the people can be threatening. It is a constant temptation to the minister to throw up a wall of professional courtesy.

But the call to Christian discipleship is the call to care, to be moved with compassion for those around us as Jesus was. Failure here is utter failure, for if the church is not a community of care and compassion and reconciliation, then it has no reason to exist. And if the minister does not articulate in the minister's manner of life this aspect of the church's identity, then both prophecy and tongues do not matter.

These texts of Scripture, then, tell us that the priest is called to be a prophet, an example, and a focus for the community's life of care and compassion. This is a noble calling, and a terrifying one.

As I admonish Bill this evening to strive with all his own strength and with the greater strength given him by God's grace to live worthily of this call, I also admonish you: do not regard your priest's response as a substitute for your own.

The priest can be a prophet only among a people willing to hear the word of God and itself actively seeking to discover the demands of that word in their world. The priest's example will have significance only if all the people are also seeking to measure their lives by the standards of God's kingdom. The priest can give constant expression to compassion best within a community also marked by care and compassion in its common life. The priest cannot be asked to replace the Christian community but only to be the member of the community who gives explicit expression to these dimensions of its life.

If the priest is made to be a substitute for the response of faith expected of the church, then the priest is robbed of his humanity and of a place within God's people. Please remember that the priest also needs to hear prophecy, also requires examples of the witness of faith, and above all, needs your compassion. Like us all, the priest does not ultimately bear witness to the sufferings of Christ only in words, but above all in the bones.

MARRIAGE: TRUE LOVE[1]

First John 4:7–10

My sisters and brothers in Christ, greetings to you all in the Lord! I am delighted, Laurel and Michael, to join your family and friends in witnessing to and applauding your making covenant with each other today. You are the doers of this deed, the hierophants of this mystery. The rest of us are here in a secondary, but not altogether insignificant, capacity. Partly we are your cheering section. But partly also we are witnesses.

You are so joyful and keyed up at this moment that the full significance of what you are doing today may pass you by. We have gathered as your witnesses so that after the haze of excitement has worn off, we can remind you, "Yes, you did it." By joining in as witnesses, we also implicate ourselves in your covenant with each other. We have a stake in it and in your shared future. As you cut a covenant with each other this day, therefore, we simultaneously cut one with you. As you pledge love and loyalty to each other, so we together pledge them to you.

The deed you do today, in truth, and the deed we witness, is not a private tryst, but a public trust. This is neither the beginning nor—we hope—the end of your romance. It is something else altogether. It is the making of a family, the assuming of a social responsibility, the forging of a public corporation (all rights and entitlements pertaining thereto attached). As shareholders in the same market, we are naturally interested in the success of this new thing. Your partnership influences ours, as ours does yours.

We have not, however, gathered in a corporate boardroom or at city hall. We gather ourselves in a church, and for however short a time and however tenuously, we constitute ourselves as church today together with you. At the very least, this gesture of gathering here means that we are

1. At the wedding of a student, Louisville, Kentucky, October 20, 1990 (names are altered).

willing to grant some authority to a story larger and longer than our own, a covenant older and more pressing than the one you now cut, a word still more public and pertinent than any words we say to each other. We gather as a people who recognize God as our Creator, Jesus Christ as our Savior, and the Holy Spirit as our Sanctifier.

And that's the reason we hand ourselves over to this peculiar ritual. Poised for action, we pause to read. Perched on the end of the diving board (Let's do it! Let's do it!), we take time out to ponder.

We take this one moment before we do the deed to listen to words other and more public than our own, words from long ago and far away, written by someone we do not know and might not like if we did. It is as though deep within us there is still a residual sense that our own words—normally so glib and smooth and quick, so prompt for twisting and turning, for spin-doctoring our lives—need at least for this solemn moment to be shaped by a word older and more powerful than any available to us.

So we have listened as the First Letter of John tells us that "the person who does not love does not know God, for God is love," and at a moment like this, we are ready to assent to that proposition—or any proposition containing the magic word "love," especially if it appears in a sentence that suggests, as all the June/moon/spoon songs do, that "love is divine."

But that's not exactly what it says, is it? The Greek text does not use the word *eros*, which ordinarily is used for the love of desire and passion that seeks uniting with the beloved. Nor does it use the term *philia*, which usually describes the love of friendship between equals. Instead, John uses the word a*gape* and defines it in terms of God, thusly, "God is *agape*."

At this point you might have two questions. The first is whether you are going to hear a lecture on Greek philology. The answer to that is swift and certain. No.

Your second question might be whether what John says has anything to do with what Laurel and Michael are doing today. Isn't marriage, after all, the wondrous combustion of soul unity, the culmination of the quest that began in attraction, flamed to desire, burns as passion, and seeks total merger of the self with the other? That is certainly what the merchandizing of *eros* in our culture leads us to think. We can recite the slogans together: there is a one and only for me somewhere, my intended, my perfect match, the man or woman of my adolescent daydreams and afternoon soap operas. All we need to do—all we need to do!—is *find* him or her, let the magic do its stuff, fall deliriously into the fluff called love, and then . . .

Well, the "and then" is exactly the problem. The product we peddle under the name of love works in soap operas and adolescent fantasies. It has little to do with real-life marriage or even with an adult life. Our attachment to "romantic love" has much more to do with the excitement of the chase than it does with the commitment of the heart, with the pulsing of hormones than with the pledging of care. Those of us who may have entered the married state with the dreamy expectation that it would be the beginning of our "happily ever after" quickly awakened to a harsher reality. We discovered that marriage is not a grand passion and a continuing high. It is rather an infinite series of small compromises and tiny deaths, less a garden of delights and more a school of service. And for this reality of marriage, the words ordinarily at our disposal are of singularly little use.

Perhaps the words of John's letter are helpful to us precisely because they are not the words we regularly use. Maybe we need a word like *agape*, or if you prefer, X, to describe this particular death-defying leap, this absurd promise, that Laurel and Michael contemplate. A new word can't do it alone, to be sure, for we can quickly pour all our usual nonsense into *agape* or X. We need a more fundamental break with our mercantile selves; we need to remember that we do not improve a product by changing its name. More than the word requires change. Our thinking is what needs adjustment.

We can begin to change our thinking by listening more closely to John. He doesn't just say that God is a*gape*. He goes on to define this a*gape*: "In this is love," he says, "not that we loved God but that God loved us and sent his only Son to be the expiation for our sins."

Now this is truly a startling proposition. The measure of love, John says, in fact the measure of our language about love, cannot be ourselves, but must be God, and that the way we come to know true love is through what we have experienced of God's gifting us, above all in the gift of God's own self in Jesus.

What is it, then, that we learn by looking to Jesus, who reveals God's love for us? We learn in Jesus that love does not consist in the wiles of seduction, for seduction conceals in order to attract. Rather, love is the honest revelation of the self in simplicity and trust, which means that love does not hide behind a pretense of strength but empowers others through our apparent weakness. We learn that love does not mean standing on one's rights and demanding consideration but letting go of one's rights and showing consideration. We learn that love is not negotiating contracts that cover every contingency and possible moment, but is rather pouring out one's life for the other in every contingency and possible moment.

This is what we learn about love (*agape*) from God's gift to us in Jesus, who lived among us not to be served but to serve, and to give his own life as a ransom for others. John continues, "If God so loved us, we also ought to love one another." And this is the word we want to allow entrance into our hearts today. This is the story we invite to shape our story. This is the covenant within which we place our covenants with each other. Life together means life for each other.

We do not—certainly Michael and Laurel do not—gain from these words either perfect clarity or full security. All of us will, after the shining excitement of this moment, continue to muddle through our ordinary days, with little vision and sometimes less visibility. As though we did not know it, as though we needed reminding, John assures us, "No one has ever seen God." That is not news to us. Most of us consider ourselves fortunate even to have heard rumors about God.

But even as we struggle within the ambiguities of our lives, and, above all, in the delicious absurdity of our lives together, even with our lives' tearing wounds and tearful healings, tragic errors and trembling anxieties, wrenching fears and clenching angers, we know that from this moment on we have taken also into the stories we make and tell each other a conviction drawn from a larger and more powerful story: "If we love one another," John tells us, "God abides in us." And, even more remarkably, "God's love is perfected in us."

Very shortly now, this momentary and fragile church we have made together will dissolve. But the word we have heard, just as the words you, Laurel and Michael, speak to each other—can continue to shape us as a gathering of witnesses, can continue to call to us as your friends, as it does to you as celebrants, to an understanding of your life higher than that of private pleasure, more enduring than material success. The word we hear and the words we speak define us as a people who give gifts to each other, just as we have ourselves been extravagantly gifted.

CONVOCATION: BUILDING GOD'S HOUSE[1]

Proverbs 9:1–6
Psalm 127: 1–5
First Corinthians 3:1–17

My sisters and brothers in Christ, for this brief moment between our individual and frantic efforts to get here and our frenzied and individual attempts to get on here, we gather together. It is not entirely clear why we do this. Why not just head for our first class or our first committee meeting?

It would be pleasant to think that something other than rote ritualism brought us to this place at this moment, something perhaps connected to a conviction that although each of us is at every moment pursuing some personal project, we are also called together into a larger and shared project. Exceedingly diverse are the individual reasons for being in this place called Candler—reasons involving in various proportions motivations concerning survival, success, satisfaction, and sacrifice. But what is our shared project?

We catch a first glimpse from the symbols that shape our gathering. We have not met in a gymnasium or board room or military ready room. We are not planning plays on a chalkboard, shouting slogans for selling, or memorizing rules of engagement in combat. We gather instead in a chapel to hear the words of Scripture and to respond with prayer and songs of praise.

Our shared project has to do first, then, with our being God's convocation, a people gathered by a word not our own but Another's, a power not our own but Another's, a presence not our own but Another's. We are gathered precisely to be called beyond our private preoccupations into a

---

1. My first sermon at the Candler School of Theology to faculty, students, and staff at the convocation opening the school year, Atlanta, Georgia, September 1992.

larger project that is God's and whose character is suggested by the words to which we have listened.

The readings from Scripture that we have heard read this morning propose an image for our reflection on that project. The book of Proverbs imagines God's female voice of wisdom building a house with seven pillars and inviting the simple to share in wisdom and insight. Paul tells the rivalry-ridden Corinthians that they are God's house of holiness, the temple where God's spirit dwells. And Psalm 127 proposes that those who build a house or guard a city labor or watch in vain if the Lord does not build the house or watch over the city. The image suggested for our shared project is that of building a house.

It is an image with immediate appeal. We have watched the stock scene of barn-raisings and house-raisings in movies like *Witness*, or perhaps have taken part in real-life efforts like Habitat for Humanity. We understand the thrill of all efforts coordinated to a single end, all energy directed by a common commitment, all participants bronzed with the sun and smiling with cheerful benevolence. For once in life, something unequivocally good is being accomplished.

Wouldn't it be splendid if, at the end of this service, we were each assigned our gloves and aprons and assorted tools and were given by the Lord the specific tasks that best suited our talents: you raise high the roof beam, you carry the nails, you read the blueprint, you bring the water? Wouldn't it be fine if our tasks here were so completely self-contained and comprehensible and coordinated?

We know that it is not so simple. We are called to build a house without having in our possession a specific blueprint and without having been given a clear assignment of duties. The architect, indeed, is not in any obvious sense supervising the job. The house is not one made with mortar and bricks and boards and nails. Most of all, it is not a house we can ever call our permanent residence.

The task to which we are called is just like that of building a house, yet in every respect it is different.

It is different, first of all, because the house is not physical but spiritual. By this I do not mean it exists only in our minds. Not at all. It involves all of our embodied selves. I mean rather that it is not a dwelling outside of us but a dwelling that consists precisely in, within, and among us, as a human community. Saying that we build a spiritual house does not suggest something ethereal but rather suggests that ours is a dwelling created by the synergism of our human capacities for knowing and loving and the Holy Spirit's empowering and informing of our fragile freedom.

It is different also because our construction efforts are constrained by a peculiar contingency. The house we seek to build here is not simply this school of theology. It is the community of the church. But the church also is not an end in itself but is part of the city that is God's renewal project. Our building efforts must always be directed to the larger project to which God calls the church, which is not to build a shelter against the world but to become a *sacramentum mundi*, an effective sign of the world's potential. And the seminary? It is a school for apprentice builders.

And as we gather ourselves here this morning for our task, let us remember that we are building one house, not two. Scripture has no embarrassment about designating God's house as at once a house of wisdom and a house of holiness. Jean LeClercq entitled his great study of medieval monastic scholarship *The Love of Learning and the Desire for God*. The title suggests the delicate yet enormously creative tension required for authentic theology in service of the church. When the love of learning is separated from the desire for God, the academy and the church alike are impoverished if not distorted, and insofar as we collude in that disjunction, we betray our calling. Without the desire for God, theological learning loses its point. Without the love of learning, piety loses its capaciousness and generosity. Lacking personal transformation, theology is a silly pseudo-science. Lacking wisdom, holiness can turn to fearful fanaticism.

We set about building, therefore, not with boards and bricks but with our spiritual capacities of knowing and loving. We set about, even as we know that we are as much what is being built as we are the builders and that if the Lord be not building, then we labor in vain.

We set about, even as we know that there will not be, so long as we live, any end to this effort, since what we have engaged is not a monument in stone but the dwelling place of the living God, a God, we have come to recognize, who is an inveterate rearranger of rooms.

We set about, even as we recognize that we build here no permanent dwelling, no lasting city, but are on pilgrimage to a destination longed for but undiscerned. And like the ancient Israelites who sang on the road as they made their way to the city and house of God, "unless the Lord build the house they labor in vain who build it," so do we sing as we labor, so do we relativize all our efforts even and at the very moment we commit ourselves passionately to them.

Yet, even with all this ambiguity, I submit to you this morning that the task assigned us is supremely worthy of our shared commitment. The building of a house of wisdom and a house of holiness to and with the Lord is in our world most desperately needed.

If the people of our city, our state, our nation, our world, need houses made of wood—and they surely do—they need even more desperately in this late hour wisdom and holiness. There is no gift the church can give the world more pertinent than to be an effective sign of how God's creation might rightly be understood and of how it might be transformed by the power of God's Spirit. But it is obviously not a gift the church can give, unless we who are, or who hope to be, servants within the church set about learning the building trade.

The task demands from each of us not only commitment but also attentiveness. The blueprint, after all, is not before our eyes, the supervisor does not guide our hand at every blow of the hammer, the talents we have to share and the talents needed for this building have not been coordinated ahead of time. And because the building we are about is the building of each other up into a house of holiness and a house of wisdom in the Lord, we must attend not only to our own concerns but also each other's concerns, must study not only the texts of books but also the texts of human experience, for if there is a blueprint for this building, it is being written by the Holy Spirit in the narratives of human lives.

At the same time, we must with equal passion and concern analyze and appropriate the symbols sketched by Scripture and by theology in both their positive and negative modes. Otherwise, we shall prove incapable of recognizing or responding to the embodied word of God as it is spoken in and through human experience. The asceticism of attentiveness, the discipline of discernment, are therefore supremely the skills necessary for the building of this sort of spiritual house.

Finally, we cannot learn from each other, or gift each other, unless we are present to each other. Are the opportunities limited in this commuter campus? Then we must exploit them all the more passionately. If what we are about is the love of learning and the desire for God, then narrow professionalism and cutting corners and mailing-it-in attitudes—to which we are all tempted—the retreat into our private projects—to which we are all prone—must be replaced by a wholehearted commitment to God's project, to which we are called together precisely so that we can build, together, the church as house of wisdom and holiness.

Such a wholehearted commitment requires of us as well the willingness to patiently endure the suffering that is inevitable when people come together, learn together, grow together into wisdom and holiness. Nothing is more difficult than this task set before us. Nothing requires a greater capacity for suffering and creative fidelity than such learning and such growth together.

Precisely because it is so difficult—for faculty and students and staff and administrators alike—we are tempted to flee from it and retire to our private projects, cultivate our own garden, pursue our individual success. It is therefore entirely appropriate for us at this beginning to pray for the strength to take up and faithfully do the task to which God calls us.

May God build with and through us, as we set about building the house; may God guard the city even as we also keep watch; and in all we think and say and do, may God be praised.

BACCALAUREATE: GOD'S WORK, NOT OURS[1]

Genesis 11:1–9
Romans 8:22–27
John 7:37–39

My sisters and brothers and Christ, the people who built that tower were, so far as we can tell, the first theologians. This dark tale of the city and the tower says something important to those of us pretending to be theologians.

But I can't pursue this thought until I do some backing and filling. This is, after all, a divinity school in a great university, and we none of us want to be thought biblical yahoos who read directly from the text. So, some scholarly diligence is due. Before we can say something simple, it seems, we need to acknowledge complexity. Time to consult the learned brethren.

Our friends the biblical archaeologists think it important that we know that the tower was a ziggurat, an edifice that ancient Babylonians used in worship. This piece of information indicates the contempt that Hebrews had for their neighbors, but it doesn't amount to anything more than information.

Our literary-critical colleagues point out that the location of this story, immediately before the list of nations and the emergence of Abraham as the bearer of a covenantal future, indicates the function of this story as a kind of etiological myth explaining why people speak in different languages and also why they don't answer when someone says "come." This bit of information is even more fascinating, not only because—like ziggurat—etiology is such a neat word to say, but because if it did have that function, its

---

1. Baccalaureate sermon to graduates, faculty, and families at Marquand Chapel, Yale Divinity School, New Haven, Connecticut, 1980.

significance might be of more universal import. But it still does not tell us what that significance is.

Then, those lovable hacks the biblical commentators have long suggested that the tale of the tower corresponds, as a kind of negative type, to the story of Pentecost. The people who built the tower were scattered, and their many languages expressed disunity among humans. The people who received the Holy Spirit at Pentecost spoke in many tongues, but everyone who heard understood that they expressed the wonders of God. This is, indeed, a fine bit of associative thinking. It may even have been in the mind of the evangelist Luke as he composed his account in the Acts of the Apostles.

That connection was certainly in the minds of the compilers of the lectionary we are employing for this service, for, in fact, we celebrate the feast of Pentecost tomorrow. But typology, even of the soberest kind, is always a little random. And knowing of some literary link between Babel and Pentecost does not help us uncover what this strange tale might be saying to us today, at this year-ending, career-ending ceremony.

That the story *does* say something to us today is the presupposition of our coming together here in the first place for this rite of passage.

We are not only people who—like all peoples—make up our stories as we go along; we are people who find the very words to tell our stories in these ancient and sometimes dark tales. We insist, often in the face of evidence to the contrary, that the stories in Scripture have fundamental and normative significance for the shaping of our story.

Thus, when we gather today to effect and observe the crossing over of some among our number, we come not only to cheer, not only to encourage and caution them concerning the ambiguous space they must cross between their past and future clarity; we come also to listen together to these tales from our story as a people, so that our individual narratives might have some better and more enduring shape than those evoked by the private terrors and ecstasies residing in each of us who leave this place and each of us who stay in place.

Now, if we were given leave to pick and choose which stories from our anthology we would want to hear at our graduation, we would likely pick old favorites, stories and instructions that please us, that confirm our prejudices, that tell us to direct the plot in the direction we already think it should go. If we were to do this, then we would not really be letting the story shape us so much as we would be shaping the story to our needs and whims. No, we allow the stories to come to us and allow them to speak and force us to wonder what it is they might have to do with this moment in the story we are making up as we go along.

How fortunate, then, that the person or committee that compiled this lectionary did not know that on this eve of Pentecost, you seniors would be celebrating a baccalaureate before graduation from a divinity school with something resembling a theological education, or at least a degree declaring that to be the case. If such a person or committee had known that such an event would take place among us today, he, she, or it would have died in a paroxysm of banality, conjuring the texts which might have been exploited.

Instead, the stories enter this moment of our story just about as they should, as bits and pieces of our shared myth, as fragmentary as we are, and as incapable as our lives are right now of being vehicles of fulfillment.

In a decently managed rite of passage, to be sure, the myth would be proclaimed, and we would dance (or slaughter a goat), and that would be that, with *legomena* and *dromena* tight as hand in glove. Only in a decadent and theologically effete situation like this one would there be a need for someone to stand up in vaguely hieratic garb to comment on the myth, and the occasion, and the celebrants and attendants, and the weather, and how we have come to this place, and where we are all going, and how to tell the difference, and why it should matter—and all this in prose so bronzed that it can serve as a paperweight in years to come.

It appears that we are not only people who are compelled to appropriate earlier portions of our collective story in making up our own, but are people who continually forget key parts of the plot and critical characterizations and therefore need to be reminded at ritual moments like this one of where we are in the story, need to hear it told again, slowly.

It is not all our fault, this spiritual amnesia, although we can never discount our capacity for laziness and lethargy. Our problem derives also from the peculiar nature of the story in which we find ourselves involved. The minute we think we have its plot down cold, another piece of the story comes popping out, like the remembrance of a sixth-grade shame in the middle of a therapy session. And suddenly the whole story looks strange again.

There is this aspect of our story that makes it more than myth. It does not only glue our lives together; its more consistent habit is to fracture them. About the best thing we could have done for you graduates these past years is to help you learn how to trip creatively over the shards of text and experience.

Another characteristic of our story makes it hard to grasp with any certainty. It is exceedingly odd. The only way we can sometimes escape cognitive dissonance is by employing it. Look, for example, at the grostesqueries we encounter in our readings today: this dark tale of a city and its tower, with its picture of a god that I am not sure I like and am certain I do not understand; the assertion by Paul that the whole world groans like a woman in childbirth—those of us who have attended such parturition wonder at the moans and screams that Paul identifies with the prayer of the Spirit interceding for us; finally, and most incomprehensibly, the lunatic shout of Jesus in Jerusalem on the last and greatest day of the feast, that whoever thirsted could leach to his side for the waters of eternal life.

I submit to you that this is not ordinary discourse. It is not the way we talk to each other around the kitchen table. That we can listen to it at all without shouting out in protest at its imbecilic oddity is testimony either to our advanced intellectual flaccidity, or to some deep instinct within us that within the dissonance and madness of this language is the same silent thread of meaning that runs through our stories as we make them up.

Thus, with no mention either of ziggurat or etiology, and with complete lack of embarrassment, I repeat now what I said at the beginning: as far as we can tell, the people who built the tower were the first theologians. They were city planners, too, of course, and if they had time, probably also plumbers. But they were certainly theologians, for they knew where God lives and how to get there.

They started off with distinct advantages. They all were of one tribe. They all spoke the same language. Their plan had the merit of simplicity: build a tower which would provide access to the place where god dwelled. With such an accomplishment, they could live secure, enjoy a fine reputation, and never be threatened from above or below.

So we hear them yelling across that Plain of Shinar, "Come, let us make bricks," and "Come, let us make mortar," and "Come, let us build." Busy, busy: blueprints to read, specifications to meet, probably builders' conventions to attend.

Scripture does not actually tell us that they were arrogant, self-seeking, and idolatrous, though we are undoubtedly intended to think so. What we can conclude with certainty is that they bothered Yahweh exceedingly, since he came down and scattered them every which way, and gave them different languages, so they could no longer understand each other, and made them study things like the "theology of hope," and the "theology of freedom," and the "theology of aging," and the "theology of committees," and when anyone would say "come," no one answered.

I am uncertain whether this is a myth or a parable, whether it establishes our world or subverts it. But the story does seem to tell us something about the difference between the theologians' project and God's project. Apparently, God wanted people to approach him by a somewhat less direct and aggressive route. Or maybe he only wanted to spread the population around. In any case, the first people we read about who had an idea of how to get to heaven stand as an example: there is some distance between God's work and ours. The warning to future theologians and ministers of the word seems to be: don't mistake your own project for God's. Don't assume that your blueprints and building ambitions resemble God's at all. This is a call to pay attention to God's project, not yours.

Where, then, do we find God's way? Strangely enough, we are asked to find it in the madman claims of the One who cried out at the feast, "Whoever thirsts let them come to me and drink." Jesus, too, cried "come," and no one came, for no one understood. Nor do we fully understand why we should come to him.

What we can grasp is that he has identified within us a thirst for something beyond our own dreams and blueprints. Besides, we are not called to understand, but to drink. We are not asked to understand how the Spirit of God can come from a glorification of Jesus that, to all appearances, consists in his being nailed violently to a tree. We are not asked to understand how from the very side of One who cries out in his death throes "I thirst," blood and water and Spirit can come forth for the life of our parched world.

But there is this: we are to believe that God's project has less to do with blueprints than with human suffering; that it has less to do with constructing edifices that reach the heavens—whether made of bricks or of fine ideas—than it does with identifying the ways that people thirst; that it has less to do with the water that we provide to slake that thirst than it does with our pointing to the side of Jesus from which the fountain of the Spirit springs.

Such a realization may also help us glimpse at least in part what Paul suggests with his image of the world's eschatological torment as a childbirth. The Spirit is the life-breath of God. Giving life is God's work, God's joy. Bringing to birth a renewed world is the Spirit's doing.

Our task is to be sufficiently attentive not to abort the process. We are not the ones who advance the work. We are fortunate indeed if we remember enough of the story at key moments and catch the turnings of the plot as they occur. We are blessed indeed if we are theologians enough to shut up and let God work.

BACCALAUREATE: CONSECRATED IN TRUTH[1]

First John 4:7–21
John 17:11b–17

My sisters and brothers in Christ, when Jesus left his disciples to return to the Father who had sent him, he did not burden them with a theological lecture, but prayed for them. He thereby left a good example for all leave-taking, especially at divinity schools, where the urge to speak—if not to act—theologically is always upon us.

We do right, then, to come together in the name of Jesus at this leave-taking in order to pray rather than to talk. We know that it is in prayer that we learn again the nature of our education, the shape of our calling, the direction of our mission.

Because we pray in Jesus' name, however, we also allow the words of his prayer to mold our own. This too is right. We have come to recognize in Jesus the measure of all our thinking and talking about God, not alone in the words he utters, but in the Word he is toward us, for the world. Indeed, our reading from the First Letter of John reminds us—a reminder particularly appropriate for theological types—that "no one has ever at any time seen God" (1 John 4:12). In John's Gospel, we have heard the same, with this only added: "The only Son, who is in the bosom of the Father, He has made Him known" (John 1:18).

But if we truly want our prayer to be molded by Jesus' prayer, we must pause a bit to reflect on what his prayer actually says. Maybe if we really understand it, we will want to stop. Jesus tells us in another place, after all, "ask and you shall receive" (Matt 7:7), which sounds like a good deal at first, but becomes a less enchanting prospect when we remember that when we

1. Baccalaureate sermon to graduating class, family, and faculty at Marquand Chapel, Yale Divinity School, New Haven, Connecticut, May 23, 1982.

really *ask*, and not just mouth words manipulatively, we hand ourselves over to Another's power. So it is natural that we should look over Jesus' prayer a bit more carefully, to be sure we want it said for us, especially that last part, where Jesus says, "Sanctify them in the truth; Thy word is truth" (John 17:17). Do we really want to say this? Do we really want to be consecrated in the truth?

Certainly, if sanctification is a kind of certification, like getting an MDiv or MAR degree, I am all for it. And if "the truth" is the sum total of what I remember from my class notes and call my theology and that I will use in ever-more-frayed fashion in sermons through the years, then, yes, I agree completely. What else are we about here?

But if we measure consecration (or sanctification) in the truth by Jesus himself, who said, "I consecrate myself for them" (John 17:19), we might well want to reconsider. This consecration is not a matter of polish on the chrome of our self-actualization. It is sanctification. And sanctification, we have learned from Jesus himself, does not mean self-actualization or self-acceptance or self-justification. It means purgation, and separation, and dedication, and death, brought about precisely by the truth that is God's word.

Indeed, when we look more closely, we see there is only the finest line—in fact, one we cannot perceive—between being sanctified by God and being cursed by God, between being put under the ban and being consecrated. So far is God off our scale, so little can we measure God, who looks to us so like dark and absence and silence, we need the filter of our humanity—in Jesus—to see God's light and presence, and hear his word.

And when we look to Jesus, we see a human person who spoke only truth, who lived only truth, and was, as a consequence, hated by the world, separated and set apart by the world that does not care much about truth, and when it cares, denies it. We see Jesus before the Roman prefect, saying, "for this I came into the world, to bear witness to the truth; everyone who is of the truth hears my voice" (John 18:37), and we hear the representative of the world in all its splendor reply, "What is truth?" (John 18:38).

Pilate's is, in fact, a remarkably pertinent question if being consecrated in the truth means in effect being condemned to death. It is a good question for us to ask before we resume the prayer. If sanctification by God's word means going the way Jesus went; if it means being torn away from my own familiar words, the ones by which I cling to myself and sell myself to this world outside me and inside me—those words that enable me to think of teaching as just a job, and ministry as just another profession, or worse, career, which can be measured in all the ways all careers and jobs are measured; if sanctification means being swept away from all I know and cling to, and being thrown into the terrible freedom of God's word over which I have no control, well, I had better pause.

It is, perhaps, no wonder that we flinch, faced with this sort of consecration. It is, perhaps, no surprise that we refuse, or at least try to defuse, the threat of such sanctification, seeing as we have how Jesus was sanctified by the truth and was separated from the world, hated by the world, and killed by the world for the truth he heard from God and spoke to the world.

It is not, after all, astonishing that we betray the word of truth in so many ways, build so many walls of resistance between that word and ours—especially those of us who have come to this place and now either leave or stay. For we know, deep down, how multiple are the modes of our betrayal and how subtle, know as well that all our forms of resistance come down to a refusal to acknowledge that we are called to truth by the word of Another.

We avoid that word of truth, first of all, by pretending that it is unavailable. We ask plaintively where we could find it in the complexity and ambiguity of our world and our minds. By so asking Pilate's question, "What is truth?," we do not show ourselves sophisticated thinkers, but people out of touch with our own experience. We have come to this place precisely because we each have heard, however faintly, that word spoken in, and to, our own lives. We know that we ask the question only to avoid the effort of paying attention and the pain of faithful obedience—which in this matter of God's word are the same thing.

Yes, the word is spoken softly in the seams of our days, and yes, we must exercise the hard and demanding asceticism of attentiveness. But we know by now the sure sound of that word and can therefore recognize as temptation the desire to have it all wrapped neatly in a book, so all we need are the references, or have it all filed in our brains, so we never have to think again on the shifting face of real life where the word is invariably spoken.

Because of this recognition, I confess my betrayal of the word of truth, when I pretend to myself that it is a truth only for pulpit or podium, and even then allow myself the luxury of lethargy and indifference, closing the gospel in a systematic (but cunning) box and making exegesis not a key, but a more intricate lock. Or, when I whittle down God's word to my own craving, fashion it into an ideology, rendering God's word as my word and my word as God's word, eventually not being able to tell the difference myself.

I acknowledge a betrayal of God's truth when I forget, as I so often do, that in order to speak God's word in and to the world, Jesus himself had first to hear the word of God and live it—hear it in the needs of his fellows, live it in response to those needs with the freedom of faithful commitment; when I forget, as I so often do, that John reminds me today, "If anyone says, 'I love God' but hates brother or sister, that one is a liar. How can you love God, whom you have never seen, when you hate a brother or sister, whom you have seen?" (1 John 4:20); and how he instructs me in another place, "Little children, let us love not in word or speech but in deed and truth" (1 John 3:18).

I confess a betrayal of God's truth when I have been so desirous of being heard by the world that I cut the word to the world's measure; so afraid of the world's rejection that I forget my fear of God's rejection; when I so want the gospel to be intelligible and acceptable that I forget the clear fact that I, the speaker, neither understand nor accept it. But I also confess it as a diminishment of the word if I make it the means of my distinction from a world that I fear and hate, making God's word and mine the same, so afraid of the world that I declare that God rejects it, forgetting that perfect love drives out fear (1 John 4:18). God's love is perfect even if mine is not, and God has no desire to reject the world that God so loves. In such diminutions of the word, I discover that I have nothing at all to speak to the world, not even the one that thrives in my own heart.

So many are the ways I deafen my ears to God's word, so many are the ways that I lie against the truth, that I might despair were it not for looking once more to Jesus.

Gazing on Jesus, I remember that it is not my truth nor even my fidelity to the truth that is at stake here but God's truth and God's fidelity to God's people. It is not my word that gives life to the world, but God's. And despite the betrayals of my heart, I remember as well John's words: "God is greater than our hearts" (1 John 3:20).

So I turn from self-analysis to the word of the Gospel that reveals still another dimension to the truth of God's word. His truth is spelled out in fidelity and loving kindness. Thus, we read in John's prologue to the Gospel, "The law was given through Moses, grace and truth came through Jesus Christ" (John 1:17). God's truth is above all God's gracious love, through which he keeps faith with those he has called.

As we can glimpse only vaguely, and at an angle, the life, truth, and way of God in Jesus (John 14:6), so we can only guess at the awful beauty of

God's fidelity. But we have been convinced of its reality in our lives. For we have seen Jesus who, when consecrated in the truth and separated from the world, returned to the Father to draw all people to God.

As we allow Jesus' prayer to shape our own, then, we are filled with hope rather than despair. We are confident that the One who brought us here—we know not how, we know not why—will never allow us to fall utterly away but will faithfully continue to shape, strengthen, and, yes, sanctify us in the truth of God's word.

BACCALAUREATE: READING REALITY[1]

Isaiah 29:10–16

Dear graduating students, from time immemorial, baccalaureate speakers have used phrases like "from time immemorial," and "history teaches us," and "in the course of human events." Why do they do it? Why does dressing in a long robe and climbing to a high place suddenly create a monster of platitudes?

Do public speakers get more pompous the more they get public? Do they think their words will live forever if they have more than three syllables? Maybe. But another explanation seems more likely.

Perhaps the way we speak at moments like this one has something to do with our being scared. Those of us who stand on the other side of the space you graduates are about to leap over, and are gathered here with you to try to help get you from one side to the other side, understand that, for you, this is simply a day for delight and celebration. But because we have passed over such spaces before, having made more crossings than you have, we know that transitions are scary. Between this well-lighted place and the next you might occupy, there is a patch of darkness.

So we do what humans have always done in times of transition and dangerous crossing. We reach down to the roots of our religious instincts and practice ritual. I suspect you would rather be celebrating in some less restrained manner right now. But for these two days, we have managed to get you washed up and in solemn garments. We have walked you around, ringing bells, blowing horns, carrying big sticks with flags on them, playing the organ and shouting and singing. In short, we're doing about as much ritual as a university with Protestant origins can survive.

1. Baccalaureate sermon for graduates of Emory College, Glenn Memorial Church, Atlanta, Georgia, May 2000.

The same ritual instinct makes speakers at occasions like this one reach for a language better equipped than their own to negotiate the dark passage between two well-lighted places. This morning, we have turned to the language of old hymns and even more ancient Scriptures. We signal, thereby, that even we who greet you from a place you have yet to occupy are also only human. We also are in transition, also are frightened, also in need of a language that can encompass us, instruct us, shape us all.

We have listened together to a passage from Isaiah, one of the ancient Israelite prophets, spoken almost 3,000 years before this sunny day. Isaiah would be worth hearing for his language alone. But it is not the beauty of his language that makes him a prophet. He is a prophet because he says true things.

Now the ancient prophets—before their words got bound up in books and tortured by scholars—were the original "other-side" people. They were the ones who walked into the palaces of kings and into the temples of priests and said, "Hold it! There's another side." Kings would be rejoicing over a great victory in war. Isaiah would say, "There's another side: look at the people killed and the devastation of the land." The priests would be rejoicing over all the gifts made to the temple. Isaiah would say, "There's another side: a lot of this is just people going through the motions."

The prophets consistently saw the "other side" because they were themselves other-side people. They knew that the way kings and priests saw things was always partial and often corrupted by self-interest. They knew this because of a perspective that often puzzled others and frequently provoked them. The prophets claimed to see things from the side of a God who demanded of people the recognition of a power larger than that defined by their success and a truth greater than the sum of their pleasure, possessions, or power. The prophets, in short, would probably *not* be the people you would invite to your baccalaureate party.

So why have we invited Isaiah to ours, just this little bit, through this tiny fragment of a reading? Because we need some help in stating to you the shape of our fear for you, in describing the danger as well as the delight of your transition, in evoking the challenge you are now facing, as well as the celebration you are embracing. Isaiah gives us a glimpse of the other-side perspective on your crossing.

Isaiah begins with a vision of people stupefied and blinded, drunk and asleep at the wheel, with prophets and visionaries closing their eyes and covering their heads. His words suggest that the world you are now entering is harsher and more demanding than college, that the skills you have learned here are necessary but not nearly sufficient, and that no matter how diligently you have worked till now, still harder and more perilous work awaits you.

There is substantial evidence, for example, that you have learned to read in a variety of impressive modes. You have analyzed ancient texts, writings in diverse languages, manuscripts, books, lab reports, equations, computer printouts, graphs, statistics, and poetry. Most of you got good grades, many of you won scholarships for even further exercises in reading, some of you have won awards and distinctions. We celebrate these accomplishments with you.

At the same time, we know that your reading skills have yet to be tested in ways you cannot now anticipate. What you will be asked to read are not necessarily going to be texts written in books, or samples in clearly marked bottles, or answers provided at the end of a quiz. The reading ahead of you involves the complex, tangled, ever-moving, often threatening world of human culture and politics.

You will be called upon to read the meaning of misery among tenement dwellers, of hatred among terrorists, of fever in a child and depression in a young wife, of destitution and despair among the discarded in our cities. So many texts whose meaning is not easily yielded, and whose misreading has great consequences. Missing the meaning of these human texts does not mean a C grade, but loss, ruin, disaster, death.

And you must do such reading on the run. Not only you are in transition. The world you enter is like a fast-moving stream; no, like a torrent of constant transition. We struggle to grasp or comprehend the complex algorithms of an ever-more-informationally connected and commercially driven universe that we call the global village, even as we try to preserve the remaining human values that make it a village we would wish to inhabit. Our world desperately needs your skills in reading.

Yet Isaiah pictures a situation where the meaning of real-life situations becomes "like the words of a book that is sealed. When they give it to one who can read, saying, 'read this,' he says, 'I cannot, for it is sealed.' And when they give the book to one who cannot read, saying, 'read this,' he says, 'I cannot read.'"

Life will ask of you, we will demand of you, skills for reading, for analyzing, for thinking with mind and heart and fast feet, far beyond what you have already demonstrated. The skills you learned here at Emory College will be necessary, but not sufficient.

Isaiah points us to a reason why the reading of reality will be harder outside this place. It is not simply that what you will be required to read is more complex and demands quicker wits and a more courageous heart. It is that the rules of reading are themselves controverted and sometimes corrupted. Here, you may have had a dull or incompetent teacher, or cheating classmate, or morally obtuse friend. But the rules for reading have been clear and consistent. For all its faults, the academy has remained to this point in time a place where the central enterprise is fundamentally what it claims to be: research matters, evidence counts, clarity convinces, reasoned arguments are acknowledged, grades are assigned on merit.

Your experience here has not prepared you for the culture wars and political battles in which clear thinking and seeking truth are resisted by those with a stake in obscurity and corruption, who trade on the gap between what they profess and how they behave, who, as Isaiah says, hide "their deeds in the dark, and say, 'who sees us, who knows us.'" You will find, if you have not already, that not all institutions encourage the growth of their members in knowledge and truth. You will find, indeed, that the effort to read truly, to act justly, and to love honestly is often a lonely endeavor in a culture shaped by the language of manipulation, and a politics governed by unreasoning bias, and a populace more attuned to the prurient than the profound, to titillation than to truth. We are afraid that we have insufficiently prepared you.

By now, Isaiah may seem to be a bad choice to invite to our party. He has called our attention to the other side of the other side toward which you leap, and the alert may not please you in your day of delight. Hearing his words cautions against forgetting the challenge ahead of you—that you will need to be more skilled than you ever imagined—and the danger facing you—that the world you enter is not entirely committed to transparency and truth.

Yet, despite his gloomy portrayal of a corrupt world, Isaiah offers an alternative reading that is still more puzzling. He declares that God "will again do marvelous things with this people, wonderful and marvelous." Despite the inadequacy and corruption of his own culture's leaders, Isaiah insists that God is doing something marvelous with the people.

And it is to this subtle yet transforming way of reading reality that those of us who care about you most appeal. Despite the arrogance of doctors, people are healed; despite the laziness of teachers, people get taught; despite the blindness of politicians, people endure; despite the clumsiness and callousness of our own efforts, creation is still called out of chaos, goodness still prevails over evil, there is still sufficient light to gladden our hearts with beauty.

No matter that we give different names to this deeper dimension of things. None of us, after all, is so much an intimate of ultimacy that we can adequately name it. But because we are convinced, despite all the evidence to the contrary, that reality is not defined wholly by pleasure, possession, and power, that there is an other side that calls us to a greatness measured by terms more stringent than those we control, we have spent our energies and time in your education, and we ask you to join us in the task of thus reading the world, and by thus reading, so to render it.

Today we wear robes and march in solemn procession and use a language more formal than our own, because we want to summon, at this point of transition, some momentary glimpse of a vision that can sustain you and us in the dark and dangerous transitions we all have yet to negotiate, a vision of a presence other than our own at work in this world, of a power greater than our own, of a wisdom beyond our capacity fully to grasp, in whose service all our passion is well directed, is joyfully expended. And so doing, we dance with delight in the face of danger, celebrate cheerfully before the challenge.

BACCALAUREATE: THE INDISPENSABLE VOCATION[1]

Acts of the Apostles 5:17–32

Dear graduates, allow me to add my congratulations to all the others you are receiving as you receive your degrees from college. You deserve praise, for you have accomplished a lot in getting this far in your life. Praise is owed as well to the parents and families and friends who have supported each of you. Together, you have done a good work.

But there is a reason why speakers on occasions like this one spoil things by adding to their congratulations a word of exhortation, even of warning. The reason is simple and compelling. What you do today is not only completing one long phase of your life—you have been in the classroom for sixteen years!—but also beginning the next and by far the longest part of your life.

This is the moment when you truly step into adulthood. And the plain fact is, you don't have a clue about what this next stage of your life will be like, or what it will demand of you. For sixteen years, you have showed up for class, done the lessons assigned, written tests, and had them graded. You have become expert at meeting other peoples' expectations of you, providing them the answers they wanted, receiving the rewards given for such willing accommodation. And all along the way, everyone has been excited about your great potential. But the world you now enter will have greater expectations and fewer recognitions.

Perhaps surprisingly, the one thing that you may have left behind forever—no more classes, no more books, no more teachers' dirty looks—will play an even greater role. I assure you that you will continue to be assessed and evaluated—tested—every day of your lives. The ones grading you,

1. To graduates, faculty, and families at Birmingham Southern University, Birmingham, Alabama, May 2014.

however, will not be teachers charmed by your unrealized potential. They will be your bosses and managers and senior partners. They will be your spouses when you marry, and your children when you become a parent.

Their evaluations will be much more demanding than those you have received from your teachers, because there is much more at stake than when you aced a multiple-choice exam or wrote a well-crafted essay. Your testers will ask whether you have really actualized the promise you showed as a student. They will not be interested in your potential but in your performance and production. Have you contributed to the growth of a business; the reputation of a law firm; the excellence of a university; the contentment of your spouse; the safety, happiness, and character of your children; the improvement of society? There is a big gap between being a successful college student and being a fully adult member of society.

There will, then, be some continuity between what you have been for the past sixteen years and where you are now going. But there will also be discontinuities. The feminist writer Gloria Steinem is reported to have told a group of graduates like you, "Don't think that real life is like college. It is not like college; it is like high school." What she meant is that you will not be able to assume that the sort of egalitarianism and idealism and sense of fellowship you have enjoyed in college will continue. Real life is like high school because it is about uneven competition, and popularity, and having the right things, and hanging with the right crowd, and knowing the right things to wear. Please note again the theme of being judged, now not on the basis of intelligence and hard work, but on the basis of ever-shifting popular fashion and political opinion and bias.

Those of us gathered today in this space also know that we are tested and assessed at every moment by a judge who is not in the least interested in fashion and is not impressed by appearance, and who sees into our hearts, and knows with maker's knowledge not just how we look or even how we act but who we truly are. Each of us at every moment stands naked before God's gaze. Each of us must give an account of ourselves, not only at the end of our lives but at every moment of our lives, for we live at every moment in the implicit presence of the One who calls us into being at every moment and who alone can demand of us absolute obedience.

I take it to be my job as baccalaureate preacher to remind you—and myself—of this most elementary truth: we are judged by God not on the basis of our popularity or our career success or even how happy we have made our spouse and children. We are judged on the basis of the disposition of our hearts, on the ways we have followed the truth as we perceive it. It is my duty as well to remind you—and myself—of the corollary of that most basic truth: you and I must make hard decisions in life, decisions concerning whom we shall obey and whom we shall not. Such decisions are seldom obvious or easy. But the fundamental, indeed indispensable, vocation to which each of us is called is to bear witness to the truth.

The Scripture passage from the Acts of the Apostles we have heard read this morning provides a glimpse of the character and cost of such witness.

You remember, I know, that the apostles whom Jesus had appointed as witnesses (Acts 1:8) had already been arrested once and called once before the authorities to be warned against speaking or teaching at all in the name of Jesus (4:17). And you need no reminding that these authorities were not foreign occupiers or alien powers. They were the legitimate religious leaders of Israel, who had also happened to be complicit in the execution of the anointed One whom Peter and John proclaimed as the righteous One whom God had raised to new and powerful life as Lord (4:10-12). The leaders demand of the apostles that they recognize their authority and obey them by ceasing their proclamation. On that occasion, however, Peter and John answer them, "Whether it is right in God's sight to listen to you rather than to God, you must judge; for we cannot keep from speaking about what we have seen and heard" (4:20). Here is the essence of bearing witness: they speak and act on the basis of what they have seen and heard—their own experience—and do so in the sight of God rather than as an effort to please other people. The court then dismisses the apostles with a further warning: cease and desist!

Since the apostles obey God rather than humans, they neither cease nor desist. Instead, through the power of the Holy Spirit, they preach to the crowds with even greater effect. The number of those responding to their preaching in fact begins to present a political threat to these religious authorities. So the apostles are forcibly imprisoned once more. This time, they are miraculously freed from jail and immediately resume their public teaching of the people in the temple precincts. The leaders are flummoxed and reduced to inviting the apostles to another hearing.

Now, when they are confronted with their disobedience of the Sanhedrin's earlier warning, Peter and John answer with words that echo those of the Greek philosopher Socrates, who had also faced trial for disturbing the population: "We must obey God rather than any human authority" (5:29).

Before the high priest, Peter repeats his most inflammatory charge against these leaders and concludes, "We are witnesses to these things, and so is the Holy Spirit whom God has given to those who obey Him" (5:32). This time, the apostles are beaten and again dismissed, but "every day in the temple and at home they did not cease to teach and proclaim Jesus as Messiah" (5:42).

My purpose in evoking the example of the apostles 2,000 years ago is not at all that you should teach and preach Jesus as Messiah. Witnessing before God is not a matter of being Christian missionaries, trying to convert people to Jesus, or even a matter of dragging Jesus into every conversation. My point, in fact, is just the opposite. It is that we should have in our lives the courage and boldness that Jesus displayed when he bore witness to the truth that is God's claim on the world and all that is in it. Jesus is reported as standing before the Roman prefect Pontius Pilate and saying, "For this I was born, and for this I came into the world, to bear witness to the truth" (John 18:37).

Indeed, we are told that when Peter and John bore their witness before the Sanhedrin, the leaders had this reaction: "When they saw the boldness of Peter and John and realized that they were uneducated and ordinary men, they were amazed, and recognized them as companions of Jesus" (Acts 4:13). They recognized them as friends of Jesus because they spoke with the same boldness and courage that Jesus did.

The vocation of bearing witness means speaking and above all acting on the basis of what we see and hear. It is not borrowing and mouthing someone else's testimony and passing it off as our own. Authentic witness in the world means taking the risk of standing in our own bodies, of occupying our very particular space and limited perspective, and speaking the truth as we see and hear it. Bearing authentic witness means putting our bodies on the line for the truth as we perceive it, no matter what the cost.

Such witness is always costly, because the real world into which you are now graduating is far more comfortable with everyone mouthing the common slogans and sharing the common prejudices. It dislikes being challenged by the truth of embodied witness.

But such witness is indispensable, because without the willingness of some among us to speak and act authentically, we are all lost in the fog of commercial and political doublespeak, we are all captive to the chains of the current conventional wisdom.

Such witness is the indispensable vocation, because it is the task each one of us is called to and cannot transfer to another, for each of us occupies a space in the world that no one else does. Our witness is required.

In light of this high responsibility, then, I invite you to assess your college experience from a different perspective.

Your best moments were not those in which you learned how to fit in, but those in which you found the strength to stand out, even if alone.

Your best friends were not those who encouraged you in your foolish conformity, but those who challenged you to be your authentic self.

Your best classes were not those that prepared you for a job, but those that prepared you not to have a job.

Your best assignments were not those that were easy to complete, but those that demanded of you patience and discipline.

Your best papers were not those in which you gave back to the professor what you thought she wanted, but those in which you argued for a position of which you were passionately convinced was true.

Your best teachers were not those who sought your friendship or gave you easy grades, but those who demanded that you reach deep into yourself to take a stand on an important question.

These are the moments at Birmingham-Southern that truly prepared you for the next stage in your life. Build on them.

Made in the USA
Middletown, DE
02 June 2024

55186521R00116